The Art of Selling

...a Practical Approach to Sales Success

George O. Emetuche

ENDORSEMENTS

Once again, George has written a masterpiece for sales success. "The Art of Selling" is a must read for anyone who needs to grow his business or advance his career. The book provides valuable insights from a master salesman and is a fitting follow up to his earlier books on sales: "The Selling Champion" and "The 25 Unbreakable Laws of Sales." Don't just read this book; apply it and be amazed by the transformation in your endeavour.

– Mazi Sam Ohuabunwa, OFR
President, Pharmaceutical Society of Nigeria.

Salesmen must understand that it is about selling the right products, services or solutions to the right prospects, whether big, medium or small. ***The Art of Selling*** provides the right models illustrated by rich anecdotes for outsmarting the competition and satisfying customers. It is the kind of stuff that you wished that was really thought at business schools!

– Charles Anudu,
Managing Director, Swift Networks.

George Emetuche in all his books so far comes out a clear and valid resource person in sales. His style is riveting. Do enjoy him again in the Art of Selling.

– Charles Iloegbunam, FNIMN,
Chairman, Asterisks Consulting.

DEDICATION

*This book is dedicated to **Brian Tracy**, my mentor. Thank you for being a Leader who leads and shows the way. I appreciate you for leading me clearly into the World of Sales.*

CONTENTS

ENDORSEMENTS | 3
DEDICATION | 5
FOREWORD | 9
ACKNOWLEDGEMENTS | 11
INTRODUCTION | 13

CHAPTER ONE
IT BEGINS WITH YOU | 31

CHAPTER TWO
CAST YOUR NET | 67

CHAPTER THREE
ENGAGE TO CONQUER | 107

CHAPTER FOUR
SAILING THROUGH OBJECTIONS | 137

CHAPTER FIVE
MAKE THE SALE | 165

CHAPTER SIX
NEVER A ONE-OFF SALE | 209

FOREWORD

The Art of Selling is a practical guide in the art of persuading people to accept a point of view and take action in a predetermined manner. I used the expression "art of persuading" because that is really what selling is; whether what is being sold is a product, service, or an idea.

This book is written by the author of *The Selling Champion* who has drawn from his rich practical and contextual experiences obtained from operating successfully in the vibrant Nigerian environment.

As Africa's largest economy continues to grow and attract sophisticated and mega players in every industry imaginable, the principles and practices expounded in *The Art of Selling* become more important than ever to would-be survivors in this market. Companies must therefore, learn how to deal with their competitors and salesmen must learn how to scope interest and overcome all sorts of resistance to progress from opening doors to selling repeatedly to satisfied customers in a trusting and enduring relationship.

Salesmen must understand that it is about selling the right products, services or solutions to the right prospects, whether big, medium or small. ***The Art of Selling*** provides the right models illustrated by rich anecdotes for outsmarting the competition and satisfying customers.

It is the kind of stuff that you wished that was really thought at business schools!

Charles Anudu
Lagos, Nigeria.

ACKNOWLEDGEMENTS

To God Almighty is all the glory! He is the One Who gives all inspirations and wisdom. I give Him thanks for making me a pencil in His Hands.

I am grateful to a great mind, Charles Anudu, MD/CEO, Swift Networks Limited, and Founder, Candel Limited, for painstakingly reading through the manuscript - and for finding time to write the foreword of this book.

I thank Mazi Sam I. Ohuabunwa, FPSN, MON, OFR, for endorsing this work after carefully reading the manuscript.

Also, I thank my beautiful wife and best friend Maureen - for her inputs in this book. Her contribution was of great assistance.

To my Sons, Giovanni and Darren, I thank you *guys* for those questions you always ask me that require thorough explanation. Each time I remember that I owe explanations to my boys, I get myself prepared to give them apt answers. This has become another source of inspiration!

THE ART OF SELLING / 12

INTRODUCTION

YOU ARE YOUR OWN MANAGER

From where I stand, the elevator to the top is, has been, and always will be 'out of order.' In order to get to the top, you'll have to take the stairs and you'll have to take them one at a time. **John Hammond**

You have just picked up an Information Mine! You are probably a salesman, or a business person, or a professional in your area of life endeavour, or someone who likes reading to add value or to acquire knowledge. I believe you want to read a book that will take you through the interesting world of Selling, which I believe all of us are involved in - because we all are salespeople.

We sell one thing or the other on a daily basis. Everyone is involved in a kind of selling or the other. The art of selling happens everywhere; knowing or unknowingly. It has been proven in many situations that competence in salesmanship will enhance capability in other aspects of life - because selling brings out the best in individuals. This position is what I have been promoting in my speaking and writing for several years.

Selling is not just about products and services. Selling has gone beyond products and services. The concept of selling is broad; it encompasses a lot of things. It takes place in various forms and perspectives. We sell ourselves, our ideas, opinions, products and services to one another. This makes our world go round. Activities of salespeople help to exchange value from one place to the other. The concept of selling transfers value from one place to another.

This book "The Art of Selling" will navigate you through Practical Selling Strategies. The book will add immeasurable value to you, to the "sales community" and the general public.

After writing the first edition of this book in 2014 and launching a masterpiece "The 25 Unbreakable Laws of Sales" in 2018, I felt the time is ripe to update, The Art of Selling. A lot of things have changed in recent times. Technology has advanced tremendously. Customers and prospects are becoming more informed and somewhat fastidious by the day. Products and services have also flooded the market; giving rise to high rate of competition. Competition has increased greatly in the marketplace. This scenario requires highly informed salesmen who will get to the sales arena and explore advanced selling strategies. These reasons necessitated the revised edition of this book. I believe the book you have here will take you to the next level in the world of selling.

Learning the art of selling is one of the ways to succeed both in private and professional life. You need the art of selling in business and in your personal life.

Businessmen who are good salesmen do better in business than their counterparts who sit in their offices issuing executive orders. As the founder of our business, my designation is Chief Executive Salesman. I lead the way in designing sales models and strategies. I am not an "Office Sitting Chief Executive." I lead the way in the sales arena because selling is a serious business. Any company that fails in the area of selling will stop "breathing!"

Let me tell you this true story to buttress the fact that selling is a practical job. Sales profession is like a boxing champion who wants to defend his title. The champion must get inside the ring and deliver more punches than his opponents - if he truly desires to retain his belt. If you want to sell, you must get to the field and distinguish yourself!

On 26th June, 2018, our company The Selling Champion Consulting Limited won first position in the Education Category and 13th position in the overall contest of Top 100 Emerging SMEs in Nigeria. A total of 13, 470 businesses were nominated for the contest that attracted organizations from all of the country. The contest was for SMEs that have distinguished themselves by providing outstanding products and services. The competition was organized by ConnectNigeria and sponsored by Union Bank PLC, British Council and Lagos Chamber of Commerce and Industry. Organizers of the contest adopted online voting process to select top 100 companies from organizations nominated for the competition.

The voting process which lasted for 30 days is a true case of determination and fighting spirit of our team. Let me also inform you that we had two big events happening at the same time that period. The Top 100 SMEs Contest coincided with our Annual Masterclass Season which held on 9th June, 2018. The Masterclass Season is usually a busy period for our company because of planning and marketing activities that take place before the Deal Day. The 2018 Masterclass hosted 120 managers and 80 CEOs, and bringing those busy people together was taxing. It required concerted marketing and selling efforts.

Consequently, I told my team that we would be strategic in the two events without allowing any of them to experience any form of shortcoming. By the time it was two weeks to our Masterclass, we already had 97 votes in the contest and I informed my team to slow down on efforts regarding seeking votes for the Top 100 SMEs and to concentrate more on the Masterclass. In execution of strategy, you need to know the action that is urgent, the one that is important and the one that is urgent and important. Some actions may be important but not urgent, while some are urgent but not important. You must be guided properly in this aspect. It is a rule to always attend to urgent and important matters first. This rule, we applied in this context. We concentrated our efforts to first execute the Annual Masterclass which recorded success, and later return to the contest. By the time we came back to the competition two weeks after our masterclass, our votes had increased to 98. Our position in the education category was 9th. The position may not bring us in within the first 100 SMEs. By the time we were analyzing the situation, it was remaining only 3 days to end the contest. Time was not on our side! But I believe in strategy. I believe in selling. I believe in top performance. I believe in hard work. I believe in team work. I believe also that everything is possible. So I gave our team a target that we should work hard to be the first in the education category and first 20 companies in the overall contest. So the battle began! The company that was at first position in our category at that time had 247 votes, and the second position had a distant 147 votes and the sequence followed that way until our 98 votes that kept us at 9th position in the education category.

The company that was at first position in our category felt it was a walkover because they were well ahead of everyone, so they quitted making further efforts - because they somewhat "declared" themselves winners even before the end of the contest! We observed their votes via the organizer's website and it then stood at 247 for a long time until they noticed our effort. Overconfidence could be a negative attribute sometimes, you know what I mean. You just need to keep fighting on until the battle is declared over. I teach salesmen to always leave the sales door open. Never close the sales door. Leave it open and keep selling. You never can tell where you will meet or exceed your target. Just keep selling! Keep doing your best and don't slow down efforts in the middle of the battle. Your competitor could take advantage of any slightest opportunity. This is one of the lessons you will take away from this true story.

Our company's slogan reads boldly: "We Know The Art of Selling." The contest provided us the opportunity to prove our competence in the art of selling. Therefore, I told myself that this is a good test case for me and for our company. The contest was all over the social media. The digital marketing activities by contestants were enormous. The competition attracted the awareness of over 2 million people. It was truly a huge event.

We designed our strategy which was to explore relationships. I also reached out to people personally. My team reached out consistently to friends, fans, family members and associates - in all our online platforms. I was involved in the planning and execution of the project. I remember when one of my facebook fans advised me to appoint a company to carry out the online voting campaign for us. I thanked him for his advice and felt that if our company that is a sales and marketing consulting company should fail in seeking for votes, then no other company could. The contest was tough but we approached it with the right mindset.

By the time it was 24 hours to end the contest; we got to first position in our category overtaking 8 companies, and among first 20 companies in the contest! That was the time the previous leader woke up. They enhanced their efforts in the morning of the last day and overtook us by 2 votes. Our communication strategy was apt. We updated our friends and fans on the go. When we dropped to second position, I announced it as breaking news; informing our friends and fans that our company has slipped to second position. I announced it through our social media platforms with a kind of emotional tone and my message read thus:

"Breaking News! The Selling Champion Consulting Limited has just dropped to second position in the contest. We can bounce back to first position if you vote now."

The message got the emotional effect I wanted it to communicate. It was that time that many of my people became more committed to the course. They saw it as "Our Winning!" Many of them reached us via phone and social media asking how to vote. The breaking news did a great job. In selling, always know what to communicate at every point in time. You must know what to say, how to say it, when to say it and where to say it. Great communication skill helps the selling.

> *In selling, always know what to communicate at every point in time. You must know what to say, how to say it, when to say it and where to say it. Great communication skill helps the selling.*

Now the time for the end game in the contest has come. The competition atmosphere was tensed up; all the contestants made last minutes efforts to win the contest. We increased our efforts to match the votes of our nearest rival but they truly fought like the proverbial wounded lion. They did their best the last minutes and tried all they could, to sustain the marginal lead; they did everything possible to maintain the first position but our fighting spirit was high. We fought back! We applied many smart selling strategies. I explored my concept of strategic selling where I reached out personally to selected friends who command high level of influence to ask them to give me 20 votes each within 1 hour. This strategy gave us edge over our closest competitor. We overtook them and bounced back to first position!

Now it was time to apply the winning strategies that won the contest for our team. Maureen my wife, who is Executive Director in our company, suggested that we move to the field to get the votes. She felt we needed to ensure that we maintain our lead by going the extra mile. It sounded abnormal to get to peoples' offices to ask them to vote for our company but it was the strategy that got us the winning. You need to be a bit abnormal if you want to attain extraordinary feat. Champions are abnormal people!

I believe that success in life follows defined principles. You need to apply the principles that will lead to success in your endeavours. I believe there is an atom of selling in everything. Selling opportunities show itself all the time. You need to be alert to notice the opportunities. The salesman needs to be vigilant to know the right actions to take in the sales arena.

One of the challenges in the voting was the rigorous process. The voting process required that voters fill-in relevant information on the voting website before casting their votes. A lot of people didn't have the patience to wait for this procedure; while some tried and couldn't succeed because of one reason or the other. So when we got this feedback as regards the challenges in the voting process, we decided to do something differently to get more votes. I know that other contestants won't go this far to seek votes; they won't have the time to go out to seek votes. They have "more important things" to do with their time. But I always believe that the second position in a contest is the first loser. I believe that our company, The Selling Champion Consulting Limited cannot be in a Sales Competition - in Education Category - only to come second. I was guided by this state of mind throughout the event. I took the contest seriously as if it was a 100 million dollar competition - because our company's name was at stake. We can't be in a contest to fail. Everything happens in the mind.

Thinking outside the box is ideal most of the time, so we explored our Influence Zone. Personal Selling is always a winning sales strategy. We visited three companies we conduct training for- to get votes from their salespeople. We were lucky to meet a reasonable number of salespeople in the offices who casted the votes. In two of the companies, their salesmen just finished their sales meeting when we walked in. They were happy to see us and I explained our mission. As expected, they all knew about the contest; some have voted for us, while some couldn't vote because of the reasons I explained earlier; the rigorous voting process. So we guided them on the voting process and closed the "deal!" Another extraordinary thing we did to get votes was to watch Nigeria Argentina last group World Cup Match in a viewing centre. Maureen and I could have stayed at home to watch the Russia 2018 World Cup Match that evening but we felt watching the match in the viewing centre in our estate would enable us get some votes from friends and neighbours. Yes! It happened as planned. We got 7 votes from football lovers that night. Thou Nigeria lost the match but the 7 votes were our consolation. Selling is about strategy, the right mindset, and determination. You must know what to do and how to do it. Selling is fun when you believe in what you are selling. You must be proud to sell your products and services all the time. You are your number one fan. You must support yourself before other people will support you. You must vote for yourself before other people will vote for you.

> *You are your number one fan. You must support yourself before other people will support you. You must vote for yourself before other people will vote for you.*

We explored relationships to our advantage. Relationship is key in today's selling. This has always been my position. The votes we got from family, friends and fans naturally increased within the last minutes because of consistent efforts. The last minute effort made us the best in our category and 13th position in overall contest. We got 418 votes while the second position in education category got 367 votes. Persistence and hard work is a great success strategy. We won!

At the time of writing this paragraph, this story was 3 weeks old. I want you to use the story where applicable to address your sales issues. I told this story in this book to motivate you to keep fighting on and never give up. Find a place this story will be relevant in your sales job and execute the strategies my team explored.

The importance of mastery in the art of selling is vital in today's world. It can be applied in business and in personal life. Spouses do better in their relationships when they know the concept of selling. It takes great selling ability to know how to *sell* our positions to our partners. Some of these positions may not be easy to carry out but competence in salesmanship makes them easy to sell. Proficiency in selling is no longer a choice. It is an obligation.

> *Proficiency in selling is no longer a choice. It is an obligation.*

Today's competitive business world puts the man who knows how to sell in an advantageous position. Ability in selling teaches the salesman how to be successful amidst competition. He does this through: Integrity, Attitude, Relationship and Product knowledge. I call them, the Weapons of The Salesman. I have applied the four weapons of the salesman in my twenty-one years experience in the sales job.

Selling just like any other profession is not an easy task. It requires a great personality from the man selling in order to be successful in the career. I enjoy challenging situations because that is needed to take any individual to the next level in his life or career. Challenges bring out the best in us. It stretches us to become the best. You need to learn how to overcome tough situations if you want to be successful in selling. Sales profession is not an easy one, yet it is one of the best professions in the world. You only need to build capacity and develop the right mindset - if you truly want to excel in this great profession.

Tough situations bring out the best in you. Each time you sail through a challenging circumstance, you get to a higher height, each time you navigate through a demanding situation; you get better equipped and more informed.

The most outstanding results I achieved during my years in the field as a salesman were done in demanding circumstances. I either went where most salesmen were not willing to go or did what most of them were not disposed to doing. My guiding principle is, "Go the extra mile." This mindset has helped me in my Writing, Consulting, Training and Speaking Business. You just have to keep doing your best in your calling. You must give life all you got. The more you give to life, the more you get from life. You get more when you are willing to go the extra mile. Normal Mile doesn't pay anymore, go the extra mile and get the reward.

Gold is always hidden underneath the earth. It's only when the ground is tilled that Gold can be discovered. In other words; it takes the tilling to get the gold. Precious stones are not located everywhere, it is only when you seek them that you will find where they are hidden. I always believe in the spirit of "Never give up." This thought process is one of my philosophies. This is what has made me a Top Salesman. You too can.

> *The more you give to life, the more you get from life.*

The Art of Selling will expose you to the sequence of Practical Personal Selling. It will guide you from when you say, "Hello; my name is ..., to the stage you say: "Thank you for doing business with us!"

This book will reveal to the salesman and everyone how to start well from the beginning. When the salesman gets it right from the period he begins to generate the leads, it will be easier for him to expand the success story to closing the sale, reselling and attracting referrals.

Businesses today have gone beyond what it was before. Quest for growth and development in business has brought about a stiff competition amongst *players*. In the 80s and 90s, business executives would sit in the comfort of their offices, expecting customers to come to them. Those business managers obviously used to think back then that they were doing customers favour by going to them. Not today; not anymore! The story has changed. Business managers now attend customers' social functions in far places; outside the comfort of their offices - just to ensure that they retain those customers. Today's business arena is for the most prepared, most informed, most resourceful and most qualified. The need to attract sales is being fully understood by many each passing day. Sales don't fall from the sky, you make them happen!

> *Today's business arena is for the most prepared, most informed, most resourceful and most qualified.*

I have also come to a rational conclusion that "sales" is an important factor in any organization. The volume of sales in an organization determines the direction of that organization. The projections companies make, are based on what they are expecting as inflow or income. This inflow determines a lot in the organization and it occurs only when sales or business activities take place. It is when you are able to position your product in the market through activities of the sales and marketing department that you will begin to think of adhering to the provisions of your budget. You cannot project or forecast your inflow or outflow in the *air!* Everything stands still in an organization until someone sells something.

Organizations work with figures which is dependent on the volume of sales made. The dream of every organization is to get a reasonable share of the market irrespective of activities of competitors. Salespeople are important in every organization. Whatever kind of business you are involved in, you need salespeople to sell your products and services. It is only when you sell your products or services that people will know you exist in business. This is a glaring fact.

I have always maintained that sales activities take place every day in our lives, whether in our workplace or in our private lives. We all are salespeople. I have proved this in many forums. You require the attribute of a good salesman to be able to communicate your perceptions, thoughts, messages, feelings and beliefs to the other party. We experience this often.

Let me illustrate this point with this true story. I once visited a bookshop and observed a well dressed man admiring one of my books. The man introduced himself as a Counselor and Motivational Speaker - when I initiated a conversation with him. During our chat, I enquired if he liked the book, and he replied in affirmative but added that he may not have need for a sales book. When he gave me that answer, I became more interested. I love objections! I see them as interest in disguise. That situation gave me the opportunity to introduce the book to him. The man expressed eagerness to listen to me. My approach may have prompted that. I made him see things from another perspective which was perhaps new to him. He probably had not heard that motivational speaking and counseling require ability and dexterity in selling. My message to him was clear; I told him that his job makes it necessary to buy the book from the bookseller. I took time to explain to him that the message he communicates to his audience is "A product." I let him know that he is a salesman anytime he is delivering his message and that his listeners are his prospects or customers. He is required to *sell* his message to them in a way that they will buy into or accept what he is saying and that the strategies he needed are in the book. In the end of our conversation, he bought several copies of the book. The salesman at the bookshop became more informed. Selling takes place everywhere!

A recent study in one of Brian Tracy's works, in the US reveals that 5% of self-made millionaires in America were salesmen at one time or the other. They had mastered selling in those companies they worked for, which made them become successful because of their great selling skills. They naturally earned higher income because of success in their sales activities, which also earned them commission and bonuses. They subsequently saved part of their income as they moved on and built their own successful businesses.

Great selling skill brings out the best in you. It will turn you into an exceptional entrepreneur, a better manager, a great family person, a successful fellow and an individual with high self-esteem. Ability in selling brings out the ideal professional in you. It makes you a great individual.

> *Ability in selling brings out the ideal professional in you. It makes you a great individual.*

An ideal salesman is the one who knows the sequence of selling. Personal selling process has an order. The procedure has the right opening and the right closing. When you follow the process, you will succeed in your selling.

Personal selling can be likened to the elementary school where pupils were taught 1, 2, 3. You cannot count number 2 before counting number 1. In like manner you cannot close a sale before opening it. You are expected to follow the order.

Salespeople who fail to follow this procedure in personal selling may not always deliver good results. You should have an entry strategy which is your opening. Your entry strategy is imperative. It could make or mar the sale. The more captivating your opening, entry or introduction is - the easier and faster you get to close the sale. You should also know that the strategy to use for each individual may be exclusive to that individual. The sales strategy you used for a given prospect may differ from the one you will use for another prospect. Customers' perceptions differ. People see things from different standpoints. Therefore, the strategy that works for Dr George, may not work for Chief Kingsley. That's what we teach in advanced selling techniques.

A salesman who wants to succeed in sales must understand this fact. This also means that an Ideal salesman must always think success and develop a lot of sales strategies. It is when you think like a successful salesman that you will believe you can sell any type of product or service to any prospect or customer - no matter the circumstance; because you will be selling value to them all the time. Successful salesmen sell satisfaction to their buyers all the time. They make their customers happy by satisfying their needs. Successful salesmen create value all the time.

The value is in the salesman and his product. The salesman's self-worth and attitude affect his selling. The higher the perception of self-worth of the salesman, the better the salesman does in his selling. The more cherished the salesman appears in the sight of the prospect or buyer, the easier and faster he sells his product. This is a simple logic.

Buyers buy value all the time. Once the "yes" in what you are selling outweighs the "no" from the buyer in the sales conversation, he will likely buy the product. Once the prospect's or customer's reasons for buying, surpasses the salesman's reasons for selling, the salesman will close the sale. This is a fact I have proved overtime. The salesman has the duty to ensure that the prospect or customer desires his product. This aspect of selling is achieved at the point of presentation, and this is done by showing the buyer the benefits in the product. The salesman needs to build capacity and his self-worth to be successful in his career.

The salesman's self-worth adds additional value to his product. People identify with success. The salesman who has a great self-esteem will likely succeed in the art of selling.

A salesman who wants to succeed should always think success. Success is first expressed in the mind before it becomes visible. Successful people think success all the time. It is this mindset that makes a successful person work hard in order to attain his dream of becoming successful. What you think all the time usually becomes your reality.

> *Success is first expressed in the mind before it becomes visible.*

Famous Psychologist and Philosopher William James once said "*The very best way to achieve a feeling is act as if you already had that feeling.*" As a salesman, you must raise your thinking to a level where you believe you can achieve against all odds. It takes time and perseverance to get to this level in your sales career. You need to constantly move on until you achieve your dreams. Do not be at a place without moving on. You can't grow by being stagnant.

Take charge! You are your own manager. The language that

the sales profession understands is Top Performance. Go get those results that will take you to the top! If you have a mindset that makes you think and believe that you are your own manager then nobody will determine what your performance will be except you. You won't have any other choice than to step up your activities in other to achieve results because you are self-responsible.

Working hard should be your style. Stay around champions. Think and act like a champion. Always think like a successful manager. A successful manager is the one who is able to get things done. So, get things done! You get things done by achieving your set objectives, by getting results and overcoming challenges.

Let your goal be aimed towards becoming the next selling champion. Get involved in what you are called to do, do not be passive; be active. Get prepared for the job you want to do, get equipped and hit the road!

The Art of Selling is a six chapter work that is summarized thus:

Chapter 1: It Begins With You: This chapter states that whatever you determine to achieve is what you will accomplish. You either encourage or discourage yourself. The chapter charges you to inspire yourself, get passionate about your job and rule your world.

Chapter 2: Cast Your Net: This chapter used the Fishing Metaphor of: Hook, Line and Bait to illustrate strategies of selling. The chapter explains that the salesman could be likened to a fisherman. While the fisherman's target is the fish, the salesman's target is the customer.

The chapter advises that for a fisherman to catch fish, his line must be in water, this means that the salesman must be seen to be active all the time, if he wants to be successful.

Chapter 3: Engage To Conquer: This chapter reveals that one of the things that matter in selling is discovering reliable prospects. The salesman works hard to win the prospect and convert him to a customer. The chapter encourages the salesman to get closer to the prospect in order to discover him and his world. You only win what you have discovered. Endeavour to know the prospect. Get to know his needs, wants or desires. If you don't know, you won't sell.

Chapter 4: Sailing Through Objections: This chapter sees sales objections or rejections as an integral part of selling. The chapter suggests various ways of handling sales objections and rejections. The chapter affirms that the greatest form of objection comes from the salesman!

Chapter 5: Make The Sale: This chapter highlights workable sales strategies that lead to sales success. It shows various practical tactics of closing the sale. Selling is an art and science. It talks about emotions, feelings, logic, values, qualities, knowhow, etc. This chapter tells you how to make the sale happen.

Chapter 6: Never A One-Off Sale: This chapter encourages the salesman to open a relationship in every sale. What will determine continuous purchase is a great relationship that exists between the salesman and the customer or prospect. Sales pitch may close a sale but healthy professional relationships will sustain it.

> *The ability to sell is the number one skill in business. If you cannot sell, don't bother thinking about becoming a business owner.* Robert Kiyosaki.

CHAPTER ONE

IT BEGINS WITH YOU

If you work for Passion, you attain Greatness. If you work for Money, you receive Compensation.
- George O. Emetuche

I once spoke to a group of five hundred youths on *Principles of Success*, where I took time to speak on the topic, Passion. I told them that passion is inevitable in the ladder of success. It is one of the sharp divides between the successful and average man. You must be passionate about what you do before succeeding in any endeavour. Passion and Vision work hand in hand. Your enthusiasm to realize your vision will determine to a large extent whether you are going to see your dreams come true or not. Your passion is your reality. Passion is a key word to success. Without it, you may not even start a task, let alone accomplishing it. This great attribute tells you to move on even when your environment seems to be saying No to you. The attribute of enthusiasm is the thing that will make you believe that "Winners don't quit." Great people are passionate about what they do. Passion is a great equalizer. It covers gaps and weaknesses. The man who is ardent about his job will do better than the skillful man who doesn't believe in his dreams.

Dreams are not just realized. Dreams come true when you put all your being into it. Your passion will give your dreams wings to fly and legs to walk! The level of what you will achieve in life has a direct link with the passion and effort

> *Your passion will give your dreams wings to fly and legs to walk!*

you will invest in it. The more fervor you *invest* in a project, the higher the chances of succeeding in that venture.

US President, Donald Trump says, "*Without passion you don't have energy, without energy you have nothing.*" Passion is a driving force. It propels you to move on to achieve no matter the obstacles. It energizes you to move on even when the task seems thorny.

A career in sales requires a lot of drive that comes from the salesman. You need all the passion, determination, hard work and competence to succeed because you need to talk to a lot of people, you need to visit a lot of places, you need to stay positive and you are expected to like a lot of faces! You can't do well in this dynamic career if you are not passionate about the job. This is why I believe that it begins with you. You achieve what you are passionate about.

The attitude of enthusiasm for what you do guarantees love for the job. Love for the job leads to accomplishment. You meet or exceed your sales target when you are enthusiastic about your job and the product you are selling. Passion for the job will take you far beyond your imagination. The opening quote in this chapter, *"If you work for passion..."* summarizes the message in this chapter. Your dream in whatever you do is to attain great heights; the peak of your career. Compensation will only get you going. Passion will not only get you going but will lead you to prominence. Yes! Passion leads to greatness.

I decided to talk about passion because of its importance to the man who makes the sales. A lot revolves around the salesman in his selling activities. A lot is expected from the salesman. Various stakeholders expect that the salesman delivers outstanding results. It is expected that the salesman will live up to expectation. It is expected that he will do the right things all the time. It is expected that he will know how to work around every challenge to get things done. It is expected that the salesman will take charge of himself and his environment. Once the salesman fixes himself, he fixes the job.

> *Once the salesman fixes himself, he fixes the job.*

The things that go on within the man who makes the sales determine his results. Great attributes we possess determine the things we will achieve in our endeavours. This is why I believe that everything begins with the individual. Nothing will change until the man at the centre changes. Nothing will happen until the man decides to happen to things. This has always been my philosophy. I believe that we all have powers to determine what we want in life. We make decisions that give direction to our lives. The right decisions will lead to the right destination. The wrong choices will lead to the wrong destination. This is the way it works.

The path to success is like the concept of input, output and outcome. Success in life is summary of the right efforts made in the right direction. If you want to get better result in a project, you need to invest efforts in the right places. The outcome you will get in a given project is a function of input and output relationship. The more you invest - the more results you receive. The less you work - the less return you get. This is why passion is an important topic in life's endeavours. It takes the drive that comes from inside to keep moving forward even when it seems tough.

> *Success in life is summary of the right efforts made in the right direction.*

Ralph Waldo Emerson puts it this way, "*Enthusiasm is one of the most powerful engines of success. When you do a thing, do it with all your might, put your whole soul into it. Stamp it with your own personality. Be active, be energetic and faithful, and you will accomplish your object. Nothing great was ever achieved without enthusiasm.*"

Passion is truly a powerful engine of success.

SELL LIKE A PROFESSIONAL

You can give yourself permission to be less than perfect, but never allow yourself to be less than professional.
— *Bryan Flanagan*

On 14th May, 2018, I called my friend and professional colleague, Lucky Ikhaduwor - on phone at 12.38pm. At the time of this writing, Lucky is the National Manager, Corporate Sales, at Promasidor - makers of popular Cowbell, Loya Milk, Miksi and Onga Brands. I had agreed with Lucky to follow him up on phone on Monday, 14th May, to conclude our business discussion. Experience has taught me that big organizations hold strategy meetings on Monday morning. When Lucky asked me to make the follow-up call on Monday, I decided to call in the afternoon because I knew he would be in their strategy meeting - if I called in the morning. My thoughts were right! When the National Corporate Sales Manager answered my call, I told him that I decided to call in the afternoon because I knew they would be in their business meeting. He laughed loudly and said, "You just called at the right time. I just finished a meeting. You are truly The Selling Champion!" He explained further that true professionals know the right time to call and the right time to visit. Professionals do the right things at the right time.

I teach salespeople to sell at the convenient time of the prospect or customer. You can't compel the sell to happen at your convenient time because you are not the one to make the order, or the one to pay the bill. Sales happen at the time of the prospect or customer and not necessarily at the time of the salesman. It is up to you as a salesman to present your smart offer to fit into the convenient time of the prospect or customer. It is your duty to prove your case beyond reasonable doubt as they say in law court.

Sales is about connecting with the buyer and providing solution satisfactorily for his or her needs. The concept of connecting with the prospect or customer is not something that should be done in a hurry. This aspect is the essence of selling and the salesman must give it all the attention it requires.

I have always maintained that selling is art and science. You must be creative; you must also work with apt information. This is the way to be a complete sales professional. Don't be in a hurry to sell but do all you can to discover the buyer and his world. Build your trust account with the prospect and customer. Find creative ways to connect with the buyer. You can help your customer or prospect to make buying decisions. You can get to this level of selling if you take time to water the ground. Remember, the ground is greener only where you water it.

The art of selling is a broad concept. Your first duty is to take your time to discover the world of the prospect. As I explained earlier, take time to connect with your prospect or customer before struggling to make sales. You sell more when you know more.

> *You sell more when you know more.*

Excellence is a way of life. Folks who go for excellent performance are people who want to prove their worth. They want to stand out from the crowd. Being a professional is a way of life. No one is born an expert. People learn to become better in what they do. The more you seek knowledge, the better you become. This is the way to become a professional.

> *The more you seek knowledge, the better you become.*

You should be seen to be professional at all times. Whatever you do in your selling activities, try to appear like a true professional. Be professional in your appearance, in your presentation, and in all you do. Buyers like to buy from experts. People identify faster and easier with salespeople who know how to delight their buyers. The ideal salesman knows his product beyond names, nomenclature, features, advantages and benefits. Successful salespeople add great importance to their products and services. They give their customers enough information that will help them make the right decisions. Successful salespeople connect with their products and services.

Being professional is a practical thing. It tells on the way you do your job. It looks at the level of interest and commitment you have on the job. It appraises the willingness of the individual in the area of career and personal development. Becoming a professional in your calling is not a one off thing. It is a journey and not a destination. You need to continue to get better. You need to continue to do your best. You need to continue to expand from within in order to conquer your world. You need to continue to seek knowledge because you cannot grow beyond the level of information available to you. Develop the desire to get better in your calling.

Your desire to do better in life is the starting point of becoming a better you. The more you wish to become an expert in your calling, the more you do the things that will take you to the next level.

My experience in the sales profession teaches me that the more professional you are in your selling, the higher you go. No matter what you were taught by your sales manager, mentor or your company, the onus still lies in you to succeed. The things you were taught might not be achieved if you don't have the necessary attributes that will make it work. You just have to be an ideal professional if you want to succeed in the sales job.

An ideal professional is a person with experience in what he does; he is competent. He seeks to know and always improving on his skills. He is effective and efficient. As a salesman, he is *customercentric* and a great asset to his company. He thinks on different ways to satisfy his customers, prospects and his company.

To become a professional in selling is not rocket science. Every skill is learnable. The good thing about selling is that we all have sold something at one time or the other even as

Children. We sold those periods we tried to keep all the rules at home just because we wanted our parents to take us out for sightseeing. We used various selling strategies to sail through those times because we wanted our parents to buy into our proposals.

I also believe that every individual has the attribute of a salesman. No matter where you find yourself, you always have something to exchange to the next person. It could be in form of a products or services, ideas, perspectives and beliefs. Therefore, it is ideal to see yourself as a salesman since you have been selling since childhood.

You don't have to be in a payroll to understand that you are a salesperson. When you begin to understand that you don't need to travel to the *moon* or learn *rocket science* to become a salesperson, you will improve rapidly. You can gradually learn and develop yourself since you have the instinct in you already. Whatever you achieve in life depends on what you have decided. This is why I believe that it all depends on you.

> *The best strategies will fail in the hands of the wrong man. The best tools will not work with the wrong person.*

The strategies you were taught still require what I call The YOU Factor to make it work. The best strategies will fail in the hands of the wrong man. The best tools will not work with the wrong person. It's not about the tools available to you; it is about the man behind the tool. It is about You. What you will achieve is controlled from within. The inner-you controls the outer-you. What will bring the results is the man at the centre and that man is YOU. Prove your worth!

Selling to a prospect is akin to the proverbial saying of taking the horse to the stream and not forcing the horse to drink from the watercourse. You can be exposed to the best strategies in your workplace, which signifies taking the horse to the stream. Where the challenge lies is making the horse to drink from the stream, which is "Selling to the prospect." This depends so much on the salesperson. This is where individuality comes in. This is where competence plays a big role. The salesman is the person talking to the prospect; he sees the prospect face to face; he reads his mood. He encounters the prospects or customers. He discovers their needs. The way he manages his target market determines whether there will be a sale or not. The onus is on the salesperson to close the sale and ensure healthy relationship with the customer or prospect, so a lot is required of him.

The salesman holds the key to succeeding in his selling. He determines his success. His mentor teaches the theory, the salesman applies the practical. His Manager teaches how to discover prospects; the salesman teaches himself how to convert prospects to long term customers by discovering the ways to their hearts. Today's successful selling is about bringing the prospects and customers happily to your side. They should be in your team.

A salesman who has mastered the art of winning the hearts of buyers will succeed in his career. Sales job is not only dynamic, it is also creative. Creativity is one of the attributes that will make you succeed in your selling. Ingenuity will teach you how to sell yourself to your prospect. Nobody will *sell* you to the prospect except you. It is your resourcefulness that will make the difference. Your creativity will make you stand out amongst competition. So start creating a unique style of selling and make a mark. Start enhancing your self-worth in order to stand out in the crowd. Be an outstanding professional if you want to be successful in this great sales career.

YOU SELL WHAT YOU DESIRE TO SELL

Legendary author and speaker, Zig Ziglar says, *"Your Attitude, Not Your Aptitude, Determines Your Altitude."* This saying explains that you cannot go beyond where your attitude has designated for you. Your attitude determines where you will be in life or career. This also applies in sales job. Your approach to your job will determine whether you will succeed or not. Attitude is a settled way of thinking. It is usually reflected in a person's behaviour. It is a tendency to respond positively or negatively to situations. Your performance has a lot to do with your attitude and the way you see things.

I have maintained in several forums that the performance of a salesman is directly related to his individuality. The person you are determines what you will be or what you are going to achieve. You cannot achieve beyond where your distinctiveness will take you. Your individuality defines you as a person. Your personality defines your beliefs which help to form your vision. Your individuality is your net worth; it tells who you are, what you are and why you are. Your performance cannot be distinct from who you really are, and the way you think or view your world. This means that a salesperson with the best working tools and the wrong attitude may not likely produce the best result.

I see selling as transfer of *feeling* and *emotion*; your attitude will propel your feeling and emotion. This feeling is deposited in the product and the salesman transfers it to the prospect or customer. When the salesman succeeds in transferring the feeling he has for his product to the buyers, the prospects or customers become emotionally attached to the products. This is when the buyer is motivated to buy. When the reverse is the case, sales may not take place.

You must desire before it will happen. Things don't just happen, events happen by design. You only sell what you have accepted to sell. I believe that every good product or service has a buyer and the assignment of the salesman is to search for the buyer and make the product or service available to him. You can't start this search if you don't have the desire to sell. Your desire to sell a product will take you to places you need to go to - in order to sell your product. The difference between an extraordinary and ordinary person is *extra*, and it's only few salesmen who have the desire to sell possess this extra, and they are candidates for success.

Over the years, I have discovered that the desire to sell your product will lead the salesman to the following:

Love for Self: The desire to sell your product will boost your self-worth. The process is simple; your desire to do something will bring out the best in you. You wouldn't want to fail in that quest, hence your thought process will be positive and you will begin to like yourself. The more you like yourself, the more you increase in self-confidence. The confidence you have in yourself will boost your self-worth and self-concept - and in turn make you a better salesperson. This is shown in the way you display confidence when you communicate to the prospect or customer. The way you carry yourself and the self-assurance you exhibit on the job will in turn convince the prospect that you are the right salesperson to buy from. Love for self will put you in the right state of mind and appearance. Your dress sense would be great because you want to impress and win your prospects or customers always. Love for self will also make you stay positive during the sales conversation because the feeling of happiness in you is formed from inside. This disposition brings out the best in you.

Love for your Product: The desire to sell the product will increase your love for the product. Love for the product and desire to sell the product has direct link; the two are interwoven. You will naturally get used to what you love. You associate with what you have accepted. The love you have for your product will make you celebrate the product, talk about it all the time and sing it like a song to everybody. The love you have for your product will make you develop interest and high commitment in the product. Your love for the product will increase the passion for what you are doing. Your love for your product will also increase your product knowledge and awareness for the product. You only research what you want to know. Because you love your product, you will always explore information on the product. It is always an advantage for the salesman to be adequately equipped with information about the product he is selling. This will give the salesman an edge in answering prospects' queries and of course keep him ahead of competition.

Confidence in Your Job: Desire gives confidence. Your desire to sell your product will increase the confidence you have in your job. You are selling the product for your organization and for yourself. Your desire to achieve this will give you a kind of confidence that will open any door. It will give you the boldness you require as a salesman. It will put you in the right frame of mind which will make you prove your point. It will make you see yourself as a brand who cannot afford to fail.

You are a brand! Our clients call me, *The Selling Champion* and I answer them! I don't know how you identify yourself; do you see yourself as a superstar or a champion? What will determine how people will address you in your career or industry is how well you know the job or the confidence you have in the job you do. The way you see yourself is the way it will be. If you see yourself as a success, it follows. If you see the opposite, it follows also. The desire you have to sell your product will increase your confidence in the job. This feeling will subsequently make you believe that you have the best job in the world. It will make you conquer your environment and the world around you. Confidence in your job as a salesman will make you do the job as if your whole life depends on it. This feeling of confidence in your job will increase your performance which will of course result to sales success.

Positive Thinking all the Way! The desire to sell enhances positive attitude. Your desire to sell the product will continue to give you inner strength even when the situations look tough. The salesman who desires to sell his product would want to think positively even if the prospect fails to buy. He thinks optimistically when fear wants to take over his thoughts because what drives him is the desire that originates from inside. Positive thinking energizes your belief and your belief is your reality. Positive thinking will make the salesman design ways of pursuing new targets and new horizons even when the environment looks challenging. He moves on to attain results without being discouraged by happenings around him. The ideal salesman thinks outside the box in order to attain his goals, he pursues his targets with vigour.

Let your target be the one that will keep your brain reasoning, your hands busy and your feet moving! Let there be new ways of achieving results and smarter ways of *scoring goals*. Begin now to exploit the *Can Do Spirit* in you. The positive attitude that is spurred from within is what makes the difference, it defines your success.

YOU ARE THE OWNER!

Every success you record depends on you and your beliefs irrespective of where you are coming from. The way you perceive issues is the way it will be. If you see yourself as a hired employee, it goes so for you. If you believe you are working for yourself even when you are a hired person, that viewpoint also follows you. Develop a mindset that makes you feel you are the owner of the product even when you are hired to sell for your company. I call it Ownership Mentality Concept. This makes you see yourself as the owner of the product. A mindset that depicts ownership achieves more results. A salesman who operates this way succeeds because his work style will depict that of a man who works as if his entire being is dependent on the job. He sees things from the perspective of the owner, which makes him put more effort.

I have heard many times the story of one of my mentors, Mazi Sam I. Ohuabunwa, OFR, former Managing Director / Regional Manager, Pfizer West Africa. Mazi as he is fondly called started his career in Pfizer as a salesman Pharmaceutical Sales Representative and rose from the bottom of his career to the Top. His story is a case of a man who gave all he had for his job. Mazi Ohuabunwa, who was once a Keynote Speaker in our company's Sales and Customer Service Masterclass shared his experience to over seventy Sales Managers. He told the audience that he got to the top ladder of his career within fifteen years because he assigned personal targets to himself that usually exceeded the ones he received from his office. This style made him surpass the targets he received from his office when he eventually reported his sales figures because he worked with vigour to ensure that he achieved the bigger target he designed for himself. His determination paid off because each time there was a vacancy for a higher position, his superiors usually recommended him. This continued until he became the Managing Director of the same company he started as a Medical Sales Representative!

It takes a heart that believes in the principle of Ownership Mentality to climb to this height in any career. His approach to the top is a workable method because when you aim to achieve the highest point, the least you will end up achieving is the standard point; which is still a safe zone. When you have a target to sell one thousand units, and you set a personal target of two thousand units and work hard to attain it; the least you might end up achieving could be the original target of one thousand units; which is still a safe zone. So design a bigger personal target for yourself; don't sell like a hired salesman!

I developed a formula I call The Selling Champion 1x2x20 Rule to aid high sales performance. This rule advises salesmen to multiply the sales target given to them in the office by 2 to have an enhanced sales figure. This increased sales figure becomes the sales target of the salesman for the rest of the month. Therefore, The Selling Champion 1x2x20 Rule is explained thus:

Number 1 represents the sales target from the office.

Number 2 means multiplying the sales target from the office by 2.

Number 20 represents the number of working days in a month.

Therefore, you are expected to multiply the sales target by 2 to have a new daily and monthly sales target.

This mindset enhances sales performance. This is the formula I promote for increased sales productivity. It is effective. The formula kills fear and self doubt. It prepares a mind that is ready to achieve results. I have trained a lot of salesmen using the formula. This is how to work like the owner. This is the way to develop ownership mentality.

When you have the mindset of a hired salesman, your outcome will be restricted because you won't see the need to put more efforts. You may not go the extra mile because your thought pattern will restrict your performance. You will believe putting more efforts should be the duty of the owner. You will see the job as *their job* and not *your job*. Oh! Nobody gets to the top with this type of attitude. Assume the ownership of what you are doing, develop an ownership mentality. Don't work like a *hired salesman,* work like the *owner salesman!*

Ownership Mentality is the attitude that helped me to succeed in my career. No matter the industry I find myself, I see myself as the owner of the job. I do the job with all that I have. I invest my time, my efforts, my talents and all I should give to make me get great results. I sleep and wake up with the job. When you develop this type of mentality, you think only about how to succeed in your job. This is the type of mentality I recommend always for salespeople. When salespeople think this way, they naturally develop a lot of interest about their products and their jobs. Their self-esteem will be apt because they will like themselves and what they are doing.

The *owner salesman* likes himself and knows a lot about the job. He has a lot of information about the product he is selling; he is equipped with product knowledge. He knows what his targets are and the ways to go about them. The owner salesman knows his customers and ways to win and keep them. He believes that the customers are the only reason he is in business. He stays innovative in his dealings with his customers and prospects. He also knows his competitors and who the market leaders are; he has a lot of information about the business environment. So, he does all that he is supposed to do to ensure that he achieves desired results even if it means doing the extraordinary.

The *hired salesman* has a lot of limitations because of his thought pattern. He thinks he is working for an employer, thus have a self-limiting mindset. He lives a life of complaints and fault finding which limits his abilities to get things done. He is always involved in the blame game. He often believes that people and environment are the cause of his failure. These are not the attributes that lead to success. Take charge! It is only when you begin to think like the owner of the product that the super salesman in you will emerge.

I have always advocated that the performance of the salesman is not divorced from his attitude and individuality. Salespeople should always embrace what I call *Total Self-Freedom*. Total self- freedom is when you have taken over your entire personality. It is when you have conquered yourself and your environment. Total self-freedom determines what you will achieve at any given time. It keeps you in charge of your activities. It tells you how to begin and where to end. It is like a compass that navigates you through the journey. Life is a journey; you need total self- freedom to navigate through life. You need to free yourself in order to fly!

Self-freedom tells that you are in control of your actions and results. You don't apportion blames when you fail; you take responsibility for your mistakes and learn from them. The birds of the air cannot fly except they spread their wings; unless they free themselves. You need to free yourself of every negative attitude. You are the owner and not the hired man! Develop this thought pattern. Stop blaming your environment for your outcome. Stop thinking like the job doesn't belong to you. Take responsibility, claim ownership of the product and the job in your mind. It is when you start thinking this way that the best in you will emerge. If you want to succeed in life, you must think success all the time. Change your thought pattern now and begin to see the job from the owner's point of view. Free yourself of hired salesman's mentality. Free yourself and soar high in the sky!

YOU ARE SELLING TWO PRODUCTS

Do you know you are a product? You could figuratively be likened to a product positioned at a big shopping mall that has a price tag on it. You are a product that requires innovation and marketing, just like the regular product that is sold in the marketplace.

I have always told my audience at various occasions I spoke as a Sales Trainer that whenever they are selling, they are selling two important products. The salesman is selling two kinds of products at any given time. You are selling yourself and the goods you have in your hands and the first product to sell is You. When you bear this in mind, then you are on the road to becoming a successful salesman. When you sell the first product, you, then the prospects become interested to get to the second product, which are the products or services you are selling. You may not sell a product in your hands when your personality is not appealing to the prospect. It is easier to sell the product when you have won a piece of the prospect's mind. The prospect qualifies to a customer when he likes and trusts you. Win the heart of the prospect and close the deal.

In Personal Selling, selling yourself is one of the challenging aspects of the sales process. It is also the first sequence in your opening. The way you smile or speak to your prospect goes a long way in the process. The way you dress distinguishes you. The way you show confidence and affability - when you greet your prospect speaks volumes. The first impression you make at your sales presentation adds or subtracts to your total outcome.

Do you carry over the worries of the previous night to your prospect's or customer's place, or do you brighten the atmosphere whenever you are in the field of sales? Sales process as I said earlier is the transfer of feelings and emotions. You must make the prospects or customers feel the same way you feel about the product. You must connect with them in a way that is convincing. You cannot transfer this feeling if you have not sold yourself first to the prospect. It is when you have succeeded in selling yourself to the prospects that they will be interested in looking at the product you are selling. You must find a way to the heart of the buyer. This is your foremost assignment as a salesperson. This is how to sell yourself in the marketplace.

A lot of salespeople get it wrong at the beginning of the sales process. They are often preoccupied with the thought of how to sell the product that they forget to attract the prospect's attention. I call this category of salesmen, Sales Mentality Salesmen. Sales mentality is when you are driven only by your quest to make sales without doing enough groundwork that will help the selling. Your main goal here is just to make sales and go your way! Real selling goes beyond this method. Relationship selling is imperative. People buy people. You must connect with the buyer before making effort to sell. You must also show your prospect the value in what you are selling. People buy benefit all the time. Attracting the prospect's interest is vital. This is what gets the sales conversation going. You need to focus on the prospect first in order to win his attention. You need to achieve this because your sales success depends on it. The attention comes when you have succeeded in winning the heart of the prospect. You win the heart of the prospect by selling yourself well to him; by opening a robust business relationship with him, and by delighting him with benefits and value your products and services offer. This is the way to create a great impression.

Beautiful feelings are transferable. When the prospect is happy with you, chances are that he will transfer the feeling to your products and services. When you make your prospect or customer happy, the chances of turning down your offering will likely be slim. You should take notice of this in your sales activities.

Your duty is to sell emotionally and justify logically. Sell emotionally by finding ways to connect with the buyer. Justify logically by ensuring you are offering the best products and services. This is the way to win in the marketplace. The concept of emotional and logical selling will always see the salesman through in the marketplace because selling, as propounded by Brian Tracy, is 80% psychological and 20% technical. Emotional selling fixes the psychological aspect of selling. It talks about relationships and feelings. Once the salesperson finds a way to appeal to the feeling of the prospect, he or she will likely close the sale.

The logical aspect of the selling talks about What Is In It For ME [WIIIFM.] The WIIIFM is the latest *FM Radio Station* every buyer listens to! It talks about the benefits the buyer will derive in the buying. It talks about the technical aspect of the selling process which includes the know-how of the salesperson, the quality of the product, and terms of purchase and so on. Smart salesmen make presentations that cover the emotional and logical aspects of the selling.

Psychologists teach that Human Brain is divided into two parts: The Right Brain and The Left Brain. The right brain accommodates emotion, perception, intuition, imagination and creativity, while the left brain stores analytical thinking, planning, logic and numbers. Successful salesmen make their presentations to delight each part of the brain. The left brain helps to take decisions, while the right brain is the one that motivates individuals to take action. Smart salespeople explore this aspect in their selling. This is why I believe that selling is art and science. You are expected to discover how to satisfy the prospect or customer.

People buy solutions to their needs and not just products and services. Therefore, it is wise to sell emotionally and justify logically. Ensure your selling activities meet up with this aspect of selling. This is how to win in today's tough marketplace.

> *People buy solutions to their needs and not just products and services.*

The salesman should work hard to win an admirable share of the customer's mind. It is by so doing that he demonstrates a kind of control on the customer's buying behaviour.

Brian Tracy puts it this way: *The two most important words to keep in mind for developing a successful customer base are Positioning and Differentiation. Positioning refers to the way your customers think and talk about you and your company when you are not there. The position you hold in the customer's mind determines all of his reactions and interactions with you. Your position determines whether or not your customer buys, whether he buys again and whether he refers others to you. Differentiation refers to your ability to separate yourself and your product or service from that of your competitors.*

These positioning and differentiation concept cannot take place if you failed to sell yourself to the customer. It is when you have succeeded in selling yourself to the customer that he will remember your product exists. Most times what sells the product is the interest the prospect or customer has in the salesperson and not necessarily the product itself! The interest the buyer has in the salesperson will make him desire the salesperson's products and services. I have seen this play out in several situations. Build this interest by selling yourself first. Try to distinguish yourself in the sales arena.

DON'T BE A MONO-PRODUCT SALESMAN

A Mono Product Salesman is the salesman who knows how to sell only one product or service. The salesman does well in one segment of selling or in one industry, and fails when he or she is taken away from that arena. Such salesperson is like fish that swims well in water and fails to swim when removed from water. I call these kinds of salesmen Mono-Product Salesmen.

What has not been tried is always feared to be unattainable. The issues people face most times dwell in their comfort zone. Run away from comfort zone! I often tell people to intentionally create discomfort around themselves - whenever they begin to feel too comfortable. Too much comfort seems to make people lazy in the mind. Robert Kiyosaki once said "*Comfort destroys ambition. Don't get comfortable.*" One of the enemies of success is the expression *Comfort Zone*. Success comes to individuals who are willing to stretch themselves. Staying only where you know, and doing only routine assignment that keeps you in your comfort zone will only end up under-utilizing the individual. You need to challenge yourself by doing new things and exploring new ways of achieving great goals.

Ancient Greek Poet Archilochus once wrote, "*The Fox knows many things, but the hedgehog knows one big thing*." Drawing insight from this thought, Isaiah Berlin in his 1953 essay, *"The Hedgehog and The Fox,"* described two types of people: Hedgehogs and Foxes. *Hedgehogs view the world through a single defining lens. Foxes draw instead on a spectrum of experiences.* These two sets of classification of people are what individuals are made of. Some folks want to be Hedgehogs knowing only one thing and staying in the comfort of only that One Big Thing they know. The other category of individuals is Foxy in nature because they know a little bit of many things, therefore being able to draw experiences from all of them.

I often encourage people to be foxy. This does not mean that they should lose focus by doing a lot of things at the same time or operate from another area different from their strength zone. Not at all! Foxy Folks know their focus and core competence but still stretch themselves to know a little bit of other things. Foxy type of people are enterprising and inventive in nature, they always want to try new ideas and new things. They fail in some areas and learn their lessons, which will make them get better. They are vastly informed because they don't confine themselves in the comfort of doing only routine assignments or *straight jacketed* style of working that encourages knowing only one big thing. Get Foxy! This is the way of the genius; it's the way of champions. I train salesmen to be foxy and not mono product salespeople. I want them to know a little bit of everything. This is the way to face tough tasks.

We recently organized a seminar for a group of professionals in the banking industry. This is an industry where you will find a lot of hedgehogs. Most of them know only *one big thing* which is the banking products and services - without knowing what is happening elsewhere! I often disagree with some of my friends in the banking industry because of their hedgehog thinking mentality. This thinking mentality gets some of them engrossed in *protectionism*. They tend to protect their jobs more than the way they protect their customers. The fear they develop as a result of wanting to keep their jobs is usually more than the love they express in order to keep their customers! In some cases, they *sacrifice Customer Service on the altar of* protectionism and avoidable protocols. This is what happens when people's mindsets are conditioned to think in a particular method - the hedgehog way!

Let me come back to my story. The seminar we organized was designed for Marketing Department Staff. The arena was charged when I introduced the topic "The Mono-Product Salesman." The topic was designed to discourage salespeople from being good in selling only one type of product or service, and not doing well in other products. During that session, one of the participants confessed that he finds it difficult to sell any other product except the banking products and services. I know he is not alone in this position, I have heard this point of view previously. This position is not ideal. I took time during that session to explain to the participants that the ideal salesperson should be able to sell any product in any industry. The selling ability, skill, personality and attribute are deposited in the individual selling and not necessarily in the product he is selling. The same individual who sold productively in the oil and gas sector or pharmaceutical industry is expected to sell successfully in the telecommunication sector - once he has the right attitude and is equipped with basic selling skills.

My 4 P's of Selling will help us in discussing this topic. I developed the 4 P's to help prepare the salesman in the marketplace. The concept equips the salesman from inception to the period he sells his products and services; it is a winning sales model. The concept will help the Mono-Product Salesman because it covers vital aspects of selling.

Let me tell you a little about My 4 P's of Selling to use it to buttress some vital points. The 4 P's of selling which include: Planning, People, Product and Performance, states that sales success is about:

1. *Planning*: This is the beginning stage of the concept. Here you determine the Sales Structure that will help you achieve your objectives. This is where you talk about sales force structure, territory design, key account management, sales compensation and more. Planning is the beginning stage of success in sales, in business and in personal life.

2. *People:* Sales success is a function of identifying the right people. You need the right people all the time. Selling begins and ends with people. The right people here mean the right salespeople that will sell the products, and the right people that will buy the products. You must find the right people. The company must design a professional procedure of recruiting go-getters in the sales department - that know how to attract and keep the right customers. This must be done correctly in order to achieve success in the marketplace.

3. *Product:* Today's marketplace talks about "discovering before offering." You can't sell the wrong product in the right market, or sell the right product in the wrong market. Today's selling is *tailor-made.* Selling is no longer generic; it has gone personal! You must identify the needs of the target market before offering the products that will satisfy those needs. This is the winning strategy of leading organizations. The products you are offering must be the right products that will provide solutions to the needs of your prospects and customers. Your products and services must be of great benefits to your target market. This is what Marketing Concept promotes. Marketing concepts is the philosophy that organizations identify and analyze the needs of their prospects and customers and then make decisions to satisfy those needs better than competitors. The concept of product is important in selling. Once you have the right product in the right market, you will get the right customer. This is simple logic.

4. *Performance:* In Selling, Performance is everything! Sales profession celebrates Top Performance.

Outstanding salesmen are celebrated because of high sales and excellent performance. Performance in the world of selling is not a hidden concept. It is conspicuous. You see performance on the go. You are either selling or not. Period!

Salespeople are expected to get things done. Figures don't lie. Salesmen are expected to meet or exceed their targets. Everybody in the organization waits for the salesman to sell something. Nothing happens in the organization until the salesman sells! This is a glaring truth. Performance is a vital issue in the sales department of every company. Successful salespeople don't tell stories of poor performance; they know the way to outstanding performance. They get to the field to fix stuff. They are outstanding achievers. On the other hand, average salesmen tell *beautiful stories* why they failed in the field. The truth is that there are no cogent reasons for failure. You are called the get things done; no story!

Organizations that employ the 4 P's of Selling will expose the Mono-Product Salesman to winning strategies. This is how to open the eyes of the Mono-Product Salesman to see beyond hedgehog mentality. The more you know the basics in your industry, the better you perform. The 4 P's of Selling kills Mono-Product Sales Mentality because the salesman is better informed to know that sales success is about: Planning, People, Product and Performance. The knowledge of this concept will broaden the scope of the Mono-Product Salesman, thus helps him to become a better salesperson.

The world of selling talks about companies, salesmen, prospects, customers, products and services and of course, the marketplace. The art of selling expects the salesman to win prospects and convert them to customers. Selling requires an attribute of creativity and dynamism. These qualities define the salesman and his activities. They are attributes that come from inside of the salesperson. He carries them about everywhere he goes. He is fixed in his positive attitude; he carries his unique character about anywhere he finds himself, so he is the same salesman anywhere he goes. He is expected to deliver excellent results wherever he finds himself - once he knows his selling environment and the product he is selling. These reasons informed my position on the Mono-Product Salesman.

This book will teach you how to sell any good product that comes your way as a salesman. You need to believe in yourself and in your abilities. You have enormous deposits within you that can distinguish you in your environment. You just have to face your fears and conquer your world.

I didn't start with sales in the early years of my career but I developed interest in the profession when I was posted to work in the Sales and Marketing Department of a Hospitality Outfit over twenty-one years ago. I did this job effectively which made me receive a written commendation from my boss. That was a defining moment for me; it was a period I decided to follow a path in that direction. Consequently, I woke up one day and decided to develop a career in sales and marketing. In the course of my career over the years, I worked in a conglomerate with interest in oil and gas, pharmaceuticals, agro-allied and fast moving consumer goods. In the company, I worked in various positions and later rose to the position of National Sales Manager for the Pharmaceutical sub division. I am now a Sales and Marketing Consultant, Certified Trainer, Motivational Speaker and Bestselling Author developing and selling training programmes, sales concepts and strategies. I have written five significant books at the time of this writing; I have also written over two thousand articles online and offline. I have spoken on various platforms; small and big stages. I have assisted individuals on how to achieve their personal and corporate goals. I am still the same individual who started selling from the hospitality industry. I could have limited myself to one industry if I only saw limitations. What is impossible is what has not been tried. Everything is possible. We all have the ability to do more. The challenge is self-limitation. Fear limits ability. You achieve nothing if you doubt your ability. Try your best and be the best. Do more than you are doing at the moment. Leave your comfort zone. Do things differently. Get Foxy!

The setback most individuals have is that they play down their abilities. You are more elastic than you think. Expand yourself and see how far you can stretch.

It is not advisable to limit yourself in one area; be versatile. A utility player in a football team will always be the most sought after. A staff who can perform in several departments will always keep his job. This same rule goes for the salesman who is able to sell any product or service in any industry. Learn how to be a multifaceted salesperson. Don't be *glued* to only one product!

YOU DETERMINE THE MILE YOU WILL GO

The road to the place called, Extra Mile is usually not busy because only few people locate it and they are the few individuals that finally succeed. Every achievement in life is a function of the route the person taking the journey decides to take. A person may decide to follow the easy way out. On the flip side of the coin, the person may decide to take the long walk to success. It is a choice and this decision is not transferable. It is your call.

But I know that easy routes may not lead to the desired destination. Easy routes often end up being a *quick fix and quick fixes* most times provide temporary solutions; that is, if there's going to be a solution at all. The solution to achieving a goal is investing the efforts it takes to get to your desired destination. There's no easy way to success. Success is a function of concerted, focused and strategic efforts done over a period of time. Success is not a quick fix.

> *Success is not a quick fix.*

I once watched an American movie about 20 years ago entitled: "*The Hard Way, The Only Way.*" Each time I remember the title of that movie, I interpret it beyond the surface. In real life, there is only one way to success and that one way is WORKING HARD. Success that didn't come as a result of hard work may require additional explanation.

You have to determine within you to go the extra mile, you have to agree within you to move on. Moving on is your duty; it's your decision and not anyone else's. Deciding to move on in the face of challenges is a personal choice. I have seen a lot of people who gave up when they should have held on a little longer; just a little while. The thin line between success and failure most times is the ability to hold on for a longer time. Greatness doesn't just happen, it happens with an attitude of determination, and this strength of mind requires self-discipline. You must work your way to the top. Keep tilling the ground, the gold is in the next dig!

I have always maintained that sales job is one of the toughest jobs around. You are expected to overcome a lot of issues to succeed in your selling. You are expected to perform in the face of challenges. Excuses are not allowed; you are required to bring great results. The solution to this challenge is to device a means to succeed. You should find new ways of achieving results. Putting extra effort will likely lead to expected results.

Working hard brings desired outcome. Showing commitment to what you do is ideal. A popular Nigerian saying says, *You can't sow Yam and reap Coco Yam.* What you planted is definitely what you are going to harvest. The rate of return you will receive in a project is proportionate to the level of investment you made in that project, thus, the level of efforts you invested in a venture will determine the height you will attain in the project.

> *You must work your way to the top. Keep tilling the ground, the gold is in the next dig!*

Start your day on a positive note. Determine that you will put the effort it requires to get to the top. As a salesman who is determined to succeed, always go to those areas that might appear not easy to break ground, aspire to meet that big prospect you are scared of seeing because you think he smiles once in a year! Doing the extraordinary gets the astonishing results; going the extra mile leads to success. Look out for the route that leads to the extra mile, hit the miles and hit your targets!

THINK IT, BELIEVE IT, DEMOSTRATE IT AND HAVE IT!

The power of positive thinking cannot be over emphasized.

Great achievements first take their form in the mind. Things take their shapes from the way we think. The bigger and better the thinking style, the more things you accomplish. The more pessimistic your thought pattern, the lesser results you get.

The way you think also affects the way you believe. Your thought pattern often affects your belief pattern. The way you think will determine if you will believe in your abilities and in the things you are supposed to do. Norman Vincent Peale once said *"Believe in yourself! Have faith in your abilities! Without a humble and reasonable confidence in your own powers, you cannot be successful or happy."* A lot is dependent in self-belief. Believing in yourself is a function of the way you think.

Over the years, I have discovered a formula that leads to success. It follows thus: "Think it, Believe it, Demonstrate it and Have it!" This model is what I call, "The Success Formula." What you want to achieve dominates the thoughts in your mind. Discoveries come by means of thoughts; when such thoughts of inventions come by instinct or intuition, believe it. You are the way you think, you are what you think. Think positively and dream greatly, believe those great ideas that you think up and begin to demonstrate it. You demonstrate what you believe in by expressing or applying those thoughts that are your beliefs. When you put your great thoughts into action or when you demonstrate those things you believe in, you will begin to have your dreams come to life. This means that you walk the talk.

The demonstration aspect of the formula is the most important part because it is the work aspect. It takes action to get result. Thinking and believing are not enough; you must work it out by making efforts. You put those thoughts into action by doing the necessary work it requires to achieve your dream. A lot of people can imagine things. A lot more can believe what they imagined, but not all have the courage to put their thoughts into action. You must follow the sequence until you achieve your goals. Once you can think it, believe it, demonstrate it and you will have it. This sequence is my success formula. This is how to make your dreams come true. Put your thoughts into action. Get to work!

Most times, your success in life or career is a function of this sequence. The more you increase the level of your positive thinking and demonstrating them, the more you have greater results. Thinking positively is a process, it is an attitude you develop in the course of time. Your thought process is the bedrock of your success, whether in sales or any other career path. The success you will record in any endeavor is not distinct from the level of thinking you invested in such venture.

The art of selling as a process is a sequence that involves some level of hurdles. Tasks to overcome are enormous, you are expected to take-off safely and arrive safe and sound - just like the airplane. You are supposed to overcome objections and know how to handle rejections; you are expected to know how to handle ego issues, stage fright and challenges you face in the field. So, the way you think is very important. You are supposed to overcome all these challenges in order to achieve desired results.

I don't *economize* words when I talk to salespeople about the tough nature of their job. Most times, when I talk about this aspect in seminars, new-comers to sales job wish to hear it's easy all the way. No! It is when you talk about the demanding nature of the job that you will elevate the mindset to the level that will get things done. Get information about the real nature of the job and its hurdles, and then find ways to overcome them.

A Soldier is better equipped to go to a battlefield when he knows that his opponent is a warlord. He would assemble the best of his armory to equate or exceed that of his foe. Same way, when the salesman is informed about the challenging nature of his job, he will raise his "thought arsenal and execution prowess" in order to overcome the battle that is ahead of him. He prepares himself like someone who wants to conquer in a battlefield. You are a superstar. You are a champion! You are what you think and believe. So think it, believe it, do it and you will have it!

Once you make a decision, the universe conspires to make it happen. – *Ralph Waldo Emerson.*

SALES TIPS

1. You are your own manager. You are responsible for your results. Be the best manager of your dream.

2. Confront your fears. Do those things you run away from.

3. It takes the till to get the gold. You conquer before being victorious. Don't give up on a prospect easily. Try and try again.

4. Sales don't just happen; they don't fall from the sky. You make it happen.

5. Once you can think it, believe it, demonstrate it and you will have it!

6. People buy what they see. Let your offering, presentation and self-esteem be so outstanding that you will be conspicuous enough to be seen.

7. Be active, don't be passive! Top salespeople are always on the move.

8. Let passion be your inner-driver. This is a sure way to greatness.

9. You are more elastic than you think. Train yourself to fit into any sales environment.

10. Don't sell like a hired salesman, sell like the owner! Develop ownership mentality; this is what makes the difference.

Let your dreams be bigger than your fears and your actions louder than your words. – Zig Ziglar

CHAPTER TWO
CAST YOUR NET

People of accomplishment rarely sat back and let things happen to them. They went out and happen to things.
— Leonardo Da Vinci

Fishing and Selling figuratively have the same things in common. The two professions share similarities. While the fisherman's target is the fish, the salesman's is the customer. The two professions also use similar strategies to get to their target in order to be successful for the day.

One of the ways of catching fish in the art of fishing is that the fisherman goes with his net or line, hook and bait. He casts his net or line in water and uses the bait as an attraction to catch the fish. The fisherman goes fishing with the intention that he will be successful when he casts the net or line in water. He does not sit and assume that fishes will emerge from nowhere; he makes an effort to attract the fish. He takes an action to ensure that he succeeds in his quest to catch the fish. There must be an action before a result; things don't just happen.

Robert H. Schuller says *"I'd rather attempt to do something great and fail than to do nothing and succeed."* There must be an activity before an outcome. Consistent efforts ensure desired results. A pharmacist who has a PhD in her field, once asked me in a seminar to inform her the professional way of commencing her selling activities, and I told her to "Cast her net!" I call this concept, The Fishing Metaphor of Selling. Using the fishing metaphor, I explained to the pharmacist that when the fisherman casts his net in water, he gets a lot of catch; wanted and unwanted. It is not in the place of the fisherman to determine what goes into the net, but it is the duty of the man that fishes to know where and how to cast the net. So, the more the fisherman casts his net at the right places, the more chances he has to catch fishes. The first duty is to cast the net at the right place. The net, hook, line and bait must be at the right place if you desire to catch fish. This concept can be applied in selling. See yourself as a fisherman who developed smart strategies of catching fish.

> It is not in the place of the fisherman to determine what goes into the net, but it is the duty of the man that fishes to know where and how to cast the net.

This is one of the strategies I recommend in the early stage of sales process. This is the first method I advocate especially in prospecting, developing a new market by way of expansion, introducing a new product or when you are entirely new in a market. Cast your net and reach out to as many reliable prospects as possible that may have need for your products or services, or that may refer you to those that would need your products.

The need for your product may not necessarily be on the immediate, but it is always advisable to open up links with ideal contacts for your products. The more you expand the scope of your prospects, the more chances you have to convert more customers. I believe that sales job is a number game; the more you cast your net at the right places by expanding your link and network of ideal prospects, the more you win more patronage.

When the fisherman casts his net wide enough, he puts himself in a better position to get more fishes. This is applicable in sales too. When the salesman expands his capacity in prospecting, he will be better positioned to know the prospects that are viable and the ones that are not. You must be on the move in order to enhance your sales figures. Increasing the number of face-to-face meeting with your prospects or customers remains a smart selling strategy. This is one of the smartest ways to increase sales. The more you reach out to the right market, the more you increase your chances of selling. You don't just sit down and expect a change. You move out and create the change you desire.

If you want to create as many prospects and subsequently convert them to customers of your dream, begin now to cast your net by reaching out to as many viable contacts as possible. Your duty is to locate where the ideal prospects are and reach out to them.

YOUR LINE, HOOK AND BAIT MUST BE IN THE WATER

The place of determination in the ladder of success is irreplaceable. If the fisherman wants to catch fishes, he must put his line, hook and bait in the water. The "action" is in the water; what is being pursued is in the water and not on the

> *The place of determination in the ladder of success is irreplaceable.*

ground, that is why the line, the hook and the bait must continue to be in the water until the fisherman starts catching fishes.

Success is a summation of apt efforts. The things that later result to success is the work you do passionately and consistently. The fisherman cannot expect fishes to come for the bait if he fails to put his line in the water. It is when the fish goes after the bait that is affixed to the line that the fisherman would succeed for the day because in going after the bait, the fish gets caught!

In a sales job, the salesman should follow this fishing paradigm of putting the line in the water. He must continue keeping on and moving towards the right direction. The salesman is like a *mobile sales office;* his performance is appraised by what he is able to sell. He cannot sell by being indifferent, he sells by keeping on. He must be seen to be moving on and getting desired results.

The line, hook and bait figuratively represent the skills, strategies and benefits in selling. The Line represents the Skills of the Salesman. The Hook represents the salesman's selling strategies, and The Bait represents the benefits or incentives in the products that will attract the prospect or customer.

You need these three elements at the same time to succeed in your selling activities. Prospects or customers don't just buy, they are attracted to buy. The combination of these three constituents will make them buy.

As a salesman, your line is in the water when you know where to go and how to get there. Your line is in the water when you are consistent in attaining your results by reaching out to your prospects. Your line is seen to be in the water when you don't give up because of mere objection or rejection. To attain your goals, you must continue putting efforts; you must fight on. You don't go to a war and quit the battle when your opponent is still on offensive, unless you want to *throw in the towel*; unless you want to surrender. Robert Strauss said, "*Success is a little like wrestling a gorilla. You don't quit when you're tired. You quit when the gorilla is tired.*" It is risky to quit when the gorilla is not tired, you will expose yourself to more danger.

You don't give up on a prospect because you did not succeed in your first attempt. You must continue to put your line in the water; you must continue to follow up. Some prospects are easy to win while some may need extra efforts. When you meet the tough ones, the solution is not to give up but to continue putting more efforts. It is by putting more efforts that the desired result would come. You don't quit on a prospect because you feel like quitting. You move on when you have convinced yourself that you have done your best. You can also leave only to return another day - when the coast is clearer; when the prospect is in a better mood to be sold to. Sales Job requires all the contacts, connections and networks. The more links you develop, the more chances you have to create more customers. So, it is not allowed to abandon or discard a prospect unless it is inevitable.

How are you attracting your prospects; do you think your strategy is attractive enough? Do you think you are using the best approach? Most times, failure in a project is usually linked to the method adopted in that venture. When the approach is wrong, the result is likely going to be wrong. If the salesman does not have the required patience to stay on when the prospect is not forthcoming, then the sales is likely going to hit the rock; the sales might not take place. The salesperson who fails in the approach of putting the line in the water may not get desired results. I often say that in sales, patience is a virtue. This is one of the Laws in my book: The 25 Unbreakable Laws of Sales. You can't succeed as a salesperson if you have not developed the art of patience.

Sometimes the issue might be from the type of bait or incentive the salesman is using to attract a prospect. The bait may not be attractive enough to achieve the desired result. The hunter that wants to catch an elephant may be required to use an antelope as bait to lure the elephant to his trap. The elephant won't fall prey to a trap that has a bird in it as bait! You need to use the right bait for the right target. In your selling activities, ensure you take the right actions in the right market.

What are the benefits in your product, what are you using to attract your prospects or sustain your customers? Are you applying the right bait, do you just apply a random approach when you are doing a sales promo - where all categories of customers are treated equally without segmenting them? Every category of customers should be recognized, and appropriate treatment carried out - to ensure fitting customer satisfaction.

It takes an attitude of consistency to get to the top. It might require a lot of attempts to succeed in a project. Salespeople sometimes find themselves in the position of fear of failure which makes them to fail to try. It is when you try that you discover. Success happens with consistent effort. Thomas A. Edison once said, "*I have not failed, I have just found 10,000 ways that won't work,*" and Brian Tracy said, "*Don't be afraid to fail. Be afraid not to try.*" Attempt the task! Don't be afraid to develop a new market; don't be afraid to meet a new prospect. The worst sales objection is the one from the salesman. The salesman *discounts* himself when he fails to reach out to prospects because of fear of failure. Self-doubt is the greatest form of sales objection.

It is better you try and fail than not try at all. It is no crime that you did not make a sale after putting your best. Do your best; let your best be good enough to win a prospect and move on to another opportunity if the prospect fails to buy. Selling is a continuous process; it's a progression and not a vehicle that is stuck in traffic!

Keep keeping on and don't stop. It is when you develop this attitude of keeping on that you will learn how to continue to put your line in the water. This is the period you develop the habit of being consistent in your sales process. Move on, don't stop, continue knocking at those doors and believe they will certainly open for you. It might take time, it might also require efforts; but with the right attitude, you will surely succeed.

THE HOOK CAN WORK AS A NET!

The first assignment of any business is to create and sustain customers. It is also important that as customers are being discovered, the business should also continue to look out for new customers. This sequence is what guarantees the growth of the business. You just have to move on with this mindset and believe you can achieve your goals. Move with the right attitude and believe that everything is possible! Pablo Picasso once said; "*Everything you can imagine is real.*" I can't agree less with this thought.

It doesn't matter if you are fishing with a hook or net; the important thing is finding out where the fishes are and going after them. What is imperative for the fisherman is going out daily and catching fishes. Whenever fishes are caught, the fisherman celebrates.

The man who fishes with the hook could also be so effective and efficient that his performance would look as if he fished with a Net. His performance may be so good that onlookers would begin to think this way. He might catch many fishes with his hook because of his determination and never giving up spirit - that people would begin to think that he has other fishing implements!

Hooks are designed to catch one fish at a time, which will naturally limit output, but net catches more fishes because it is designed that way. The net has the tendency of reaching to other areas when it is cast. It is natural that fishing with net has the capacity to catch more fishes than the hook. However this analogy may not necessarily be the case of a determined fisherman who uses line, hook and bait. His performance is always outstanding because what motivates him is his drive to catch more fishes. His nature will of course increase his performance because he is determined to go the extra mile in order to achieve results. He is willing to apply techniques that will increase his output. He might resort to putting several lines in the water at the same time as a strategy of increasing his output.

In my teaching in the concept of Fishing Metaphor of Selling, I have always maintained that the tool you use in your fishing is not as important as what drives you from within. The real you reside within. The determinant of your outcome emanates from the inside. This happens in real life situations. Abundant resources may not lead to success. I believe that a lot depends on the individual managing the resources. Everyone has the capacity to determine how he or she will end. This is not necessarily a function of the environment. I believe that the environment is a means to an end, but not an end in itself. I have always maintained that the individual residing in the environment can conquer his environment to make his dreams come true. The deposits within is beyond what is in the environment. It is advisable that you understand this concept.

The materials available to each individual may differ, just as individuals differ in situations. Some individuals have abundant means that they can afford advanced fishing implements while the case may be different in other situations.

I want to introduce this line of thought because tools available in organizations to execute planned actions vary. The capacity of an organization will determine whether they will fish with line, hook, net or other advanced implements. Organizations are expected to perform according to its capacity. Some salesmen make the mistake of getting themselves involved in unnecessary comparison that is counter-productive - by comparing their organizations with another. If your organization is not big enough to provide the type of tools you think you desire; just like the case of the fisherman who fishes with the line and not net or advanced implements; then it's your duty to work hard to take your organization to the height that will get them the type of tools you desire! A teacher was once a pupil. A coach was once a learner. Ideal success is

> A teacher was once a pupil. A coach was once a learner. Ideal success is a journey that usually begins small.

a journey that usually begins small. Most big organizations started small. I once read the inspiring story of Samsung; the story of their little beginnings is encouraging. It is your duty as a salesman to take your company to greater heights by meeting and exceeding your sales targets.

I emphasize this message to salespeople anywhere I go. Your result could be so good that it would be easy for your organization to begin to fish with advanced mechanism. The enormous result you record could shoot up your small company to the top. Don't complain that your utility vehicle is not the latest model, or that you don't have all the needed sales promotional materials, or that your promotion campaign is not yet in the electronic or print media. These things are good but the question is: Are you doing your part as a salesman? My twenty-one years experience in the sales profession teaches me that most times - the salesmen who complain about inadequate tools are the ones not doing enough work in the field. They just make excuses for poor performance. Salesmen in this category end up as average salespeople. They don't go far in the profession. Do your best in the field and give market information to your company for appropriate actions. Marketing activity helps selling activity. We all know this fact but don't allow lack of it, or inadequate marketing activities by your company to determine your level of efforts in the field. This is the case I want to make here.

Most salesmen look at what their competitors are doing in these areas and use such excuses as reason for poor performance. Your competitors might have more *financial muscle* than your company to be able to launch media campaigns when your company is yet to do so. This situation should not be an excuse for you not to do your job well and get the desired result.

A president of a company once fired a salesman during an in-house training our company organized for his firm. The said salesman was more interested in comparing his company with their competitors and refused to explore the tools available to him. He was more concerned with the tools they didn't have than exploring to his advantage the ones provided for him. The president of the company later explained to me that he took that drastic decision because he didn't want to have people with the wrong mindset in his sales team. Stop comparing your competitors with your company; you can take your company to the top!

It's ideal to get information about your competitors and your industry but don't use such information as a reason for poor sales. Let the information you garnered put you in the right frame of mind to achieve results and not the other way round. Discover other affordable ways of attaining results. Make the difference, your performance can change a lot of things.

Let me use this true story to support my point. Our company once got a job to assist a company position their product in the market. The company introduced a new division in their business that imports and distributes tomatoes. Part of the brief we got was to recruit and train salespeople for the assignment since it's a new segment in their business. We came in, conducted the recruitment exercise and training as planned. We also introduced sales structure to get things going.

The challenge we observed was that the company was not financially disposed to undertake all the recommended marketing activities. They had just concluded the registration process of the new business venture and moved into a new furnished office space. They had also imported the first consignments of tomatoes within this period which they had paid for in full. Furthermore, they acquired a few salesmen's vehicles but the vehicles were not enough for all the people in the sales team. The marketing aspect of the job got its share of the challenge. They could not afford to engage in media promotion because of cost. We found out that they didn't have all the means but they desired to turn things around for good! They knew they needed a thorough sales and marketing consulting firm to sail through that situation and they came to us.

This situation was the type that required more action and less talk, and so we decided to start with training and mentoring to instill the right attitude in the salesmen. We designed tailor-to-fit training topics that would enable us achieve our aim. We used the fishing metaphor of line and net to drive home the message. The training and mentoring sessions were attitude based with emphasis on passion, excellence, performance, and determination. We prepared deliberate topics to prepare their minds on how to overcome the challenges ahead. We desired to build a sales team that would perform without necessarily relying on tools only; we needed a team that could reach the sky without wings! We considered it necessary to assemble a team that could fish with hook and still get the same result that comes from fishing with net! We wanted them to believe they could start small and grow big.

Consequently, we prepared a team that saw themselves as the main factor for success.

We also devised a means to work around the marketing activities by using more of "Below the line" promotion strategy. We didn't use television because it was expensive. However, we designed strategies to visit public events and trade shows that would be affordable to promote the tomatoes. We gave sales incentives to wholesalers and distributors of the product. We ensured efficient product delivery. Salespeople who didn't have vehicles went out and got orders and came back to ask for delivery to those customers. We made sure that we utilized the available vehicles to its optimal capacity; every customer's requisition was attended to. The responsibility of the salespeople who were not assigned vehicles was to go and get supply requests from customers. When they did, we made sure the deliveries were done within the agreed time. The sales team was equipped mentally to overcome their challenges. These efforts continued for a period of seven months and the sales team positioned the product so well that it became popular in the market. The company was so happy with the team that they were given necessary tools the subsequent business year. The sales team then received bonuses and sales commission for their performance.

The company's financial status improved because of high sales, and they were able to promote the product in a popular TV Programme within the second quarter of the subsequent year. Attaining success in life is a gradual process. You need to be strategic in your actions; knowing the right things to do at every given time.

Your hook can be your net! What makes the difference is your attitude to work. Your attitude can change a lot of things. Your attitude can fill a lot of gaps. Your attitude can change the equation. Your attitude to work is what will make the difference. Attitude is not just everything; it is the only thing! It makes the difference; it is the major denominator! It determines what will be and what will not. What you invest in a project determines what you will get. The way you see things is the way it will be. The way you think is the way you will act, you can't get beyond where your attitude will take you. The sales team in the story succeeded because they took the decision to succeed. They didn't wait for their situation to determine what their result would be. They didn't wait until their company supplied all the tools for work; they took their destiny in their hands! You too can do this. Change your attitude to work and you will change your result.

CAST YOUR NET WHERE THE FISHES ARE

Vision determines direction. Where there is no vision, people lose direction. Define your vision and determine your direction. Vision tells you where to go and Mission provides the vehicle to get there. Successful people wake up with a definite direction. They know where they are going and how to get there. They know the hurdles on the way and how to navigate through the rough path. They know their target and ways to approach it. They move with direction in whatever they do.

> *Vision determines direction. Where there is no vision, people lose direction.*

In order to be successful in your selling, you must know where to go and how to get there. You don't just wake up and set out as a sheep without a shepherd. Develop a compass that will be your guide. Always put your schedule on paper and move with a direction. Know where your ideal prospects are and determine how to reach them. Develop a sales plan that tells you what to do at every given time. Your sales plan is your sales compass. It gives you direction.

The fisherman who puts his line in the wrong place will not attract fishes even if the line, hook and the bait stays several days. I like using the, "Casting of Net metaphor" to drive home this message to salespeople. The questions that should come to your mind as a salesman before you begin your job are, "Who needs my products, Where should I find my likely prospects and How and What do I do to get to the people that may need my products or services?" It is when you know where you are going, that you will know how to navigate there.

This stage of selling is crucial. You need to know where the market is and how to move in. You need to know who needs your products or services, you need to know how and when to reach your prospects. A good example is the pharmaceutical industry in Lagos, Nigeria. A salesman who operates in the pharmaceutical industry in Lagos is expected to know the wholesale market in Idumota. This is a market where you have a cluster of businesspeople who deal in pharmaceuticals. According to the Pharmaceutical Manufacturing Group and Manufacturers Association of Nigeria, PMG- MAN, Nigeria is responsible for 60% of medicine consumed in the ECOWAS by volume.

Practice has also shown that Idumota market accounts for major market shares in medicine consumed in Nigeria by volume. The market also controls wholesale supplies of pharmaceuticals in Lagos and is one of the three major markets for pharmaceutical products in Nigeria. The other two include Bridge Head market in Onitsha and the Drug market in Kano. A salesman operating in this setting should seek to know these vital markets. He should know the buying pattern of the markets, who buys what, when and how? The salesman in this environment should also know all the hospitals and where they are located, and also have a data base of all the doctors and pharmacists - which are the professionals who prescribe and dispense the drugs including details of Patent Dealers Associations. He should get each group's meeting days. He should also know leaders of strategic teams that will help him in product positioning.

When you cast your net, make sure you know where the fishes are found, don't just cast a *vague* net, cast your net on the target. Put your line, hook and bait strategically, don't leave your line where it will stay without catching a fish. That will be effort in futility.

This also goes for any other industry, salespeople should find out the contacts that control the marketplace in any industry they find themselves. Every market has its leaders; these groups of people or businesses define the direction of activities. This set gives direction to where the market is heading. Salesmen are supposed to know where these important people are, and how they think. Salespeople should be proactive. They are supposed to go out and happen to things, they should discover the *heavy weights* in their industries and begin to achieve great results.

When you learn the strategy of casting your net where the fishes are located, then you are on your way to becoming a top salesman. Be strategic in your duty, work smartly and be result oriented. You can't go wrong when you have these attributes. The world of today's business is looking for go-getters; businesses are looking for individuals who will deliver expected results, people who will not give *beautiful reasons* for failing. Make the difference; cast your net where you can find fishes. This is what will make you stand out in the crowd.

WHO, WHERE, WHY, WHEN, WHAT ARE AS IMPORTANT AS HOW

On 10th July, 2018, our client, a leading player in the Fast Moving Consumer Goods industry in Nigeria appointed us for marketing research and training of their staff. They started soap making line in their company and wanted us to conduct marketing research and train their sales team in that regard. They wanted us to ascertain the performance of their products in the market and advise them on the way to go. Their ranges of soap were already in the market and their sales team was doing their best but the company wanted to increase their market share, thus the need to invite us.

We carried out the marketing research that lasted for days and discovered apt marketing information the company needed for strategic decision making. One of the respondents at Mushin Market in Lagos spent 15 minutes with me to inform about competitors' activities and general market information and how our client could do better in the market. Of course, I couldn't have got that vital information if not for my friendly entry strategy. She later confessed that she didn't know why she gave me all the information and I replied humorously that it's because I am a good man and we laughed over it. As I said earlier in this book, there is selling in everything. You must be alert to know how to go about it. The marketing research we conducted enabled us information on who buys from the company, why they buy, when they buy and so on. It also enabled us garner information on the people who weren't buying, and why they don't buy. We got relevant information about buying behaviour of the market. You must discover before you conquer. Information is imperative in selling. You must know the thinking and acting pattern of the marketplace. You must ask relevant questions that will give you apt direction.

> *You must discover before you conquer. Information is imperative in selling. You must know the thinking and acting pattern of the marketplace.*

I once attended Brian Tracy's business seminar where he used the sound made by an Owl which sounds like "WHO," to illustrate that salespeople should know who their customers are.

I believe that salespeople should know their environment and what happens there. You should know who buys your product, why they buy your product and when they buy your products or services. Your knowledge of customers' behaviour tells you what to do next. The information you have about your customer's buying pattern will guide you on the next line of action just like the case in the marketing research we conducted for the FMCG Company. The information we got during the marketing research helped us to design the training programme that fit the needs of our clients.

As a salesman who desires to be to the top, your duty is to find out Why, When, Where, Who, What and How of the prospect or customer. This is what I call: The Five Ws and H of Selling. You need to know *Why* the customer is buying and *Why* the prospect has not decided to buy yet. Know also *When* the customers will buy next or *When* to reach out to them. You are expected to know *Where* to find the right people you need to sell to and *Who* takes vital decisions when you get there. Also, you need to get information about *What* your customers and prospects need. Find out what your competitors are doing and invent ways to do it better. When you are through with the five Ws, then you ask: *How* do I get better in my selling, how do I attain the needs of the buyers? How do I attract prospects? How do I convert prospects to customers and how do I sustain them? This is the essence of real selling.

Things don't just happen, things are made to happen. When you apply the five Ws and H of selling, it becomes easier to take off. Your starting point becomes firm. Your direction becomes clearer. Don't be like an average salesman who wakes up daily without a direction. Sales Job is a career that requires defined direction. You can't get to the field without determining how to start and why you are starting there. You should know from home the prospects you are to reach on a given day and why you want to reach out to them. You should also know how to start when you get there. This is not rocket science; it's just being a little organized and it's doable too.

Success in your sales job is a function of your level of commitment. Your level of success is a function of the level of efforts you invested in the job. It takes commitment, interest and effort to connect with a prospect or customer. Connecting with a prospect requires a little effort and it takes the organized salesperson to get this done. Knowing more about your prospect or customer and his buying behaviour makes it easier for the salesman. It positions the salesman to know the best action to take at any given time. When you anticipate an action, you will position yourself on the best way to go about it. When you have relevant information about your prospects and connect with them professionally, then you are on your way to the top!

People buy when they have a relaxed mind. When you have information on the Five Ws and H of Selling, the prospect would be at home with you because your prospecting is likely going to come from an angle that will put you in charge. The salesperson will be speaking from a standpoint of someone who has detailed information about the prospect and the environment. Apt information is imperative in today's selling. Scan your sales environment to get relevant information that will make you succeed in the marketplace. This is your duty as a salesman.

IF YOU FAIL TODAY, TRY AGAIN TOMORROW

I believe that the harder you work, the luckier you become. Luck often happens to people who work hard. Jesse Jackson once said, "*If you fall behind, run faster. Never give up, never surrender, and rise up against the odds.*" If you give up because you didn't succeed today and fail to try again tomorrow, then you have lost the battle! Try again when you fail. Try new ways and other workable options. Review your approach and do it again. Quitting is no longer a viable option. You must do something to achieve a good result. You must do your best and your best must be good enough.

> *Champions keep moving the vehicle even when they don't have petrol in their tanks. Inspire yourself to win!*

Jeffrey James, a former US Ambassador in Iraq once said on a CNN interview that, "*Doing nothing is always not an option.*" You must work out ways to get things done. You must keep moving forward towards the right direction. Champions keep moving the vehicle even when they don't have petrol in their tanks. Inspire yourself to win! The place of determination is the ladder of success is irreplaceable.

Your focus in selling is to discover how to be on the right path. Often times, when you start the right way in any project, you will likely create better chances of ending successfully. You need to discover the best way to start any project that will guarantee your success in that project. The dream of every man or woman is to succeed. The farmer who cultivates wishes to reap bountifully, this is why the farmer is happy when his seedlings germinate and bear fruits. The hunter prays to come back each day successful. He wishes to hunt down as many animals as possible. The same goes to the fisherman; he expects his net to be filled with various types of fishes - he spreads his net wide and expects it to yield awesome result. The businessman wants to smile to the bank always. He wakes up daily believing in his projections, strategies and business permutations; believing he will conquer his day. The student wants to be the best in his or her class. That's why he or she reads aptly to get ready for the best result. The list is countless; it goes on and on. These assumptions are immeasurable. Everybody want to succeed, nobody prays to fail. People expect one great outcome or the other in their endeavours. These expectations are only natural.

However, expectations do not always come the way they are wished. You might prepare your mind for the best, only to experience the unexpected disappointment. On some occasions, you are convinced that you did your best while in some cases there would be room for improvement. This situation is not the end of the road; it is not a prison sentence.

People fail only to bounce back later. Countries experience economic recession and get back stronger. What determines whether you have failed or not is your attitude towards the circumstance. Sometimes, things might decide not to work out naturally even when you have put in your best.

Fishes may decide to "travel" the day the fisherman casts his net into the water! Unexpected things might just happen naturally sometimes. These happenings shouldn't discourage you to stop trying your best next time. Your failure today does not mean that you will also fail tomorrow. Failure is an integral part of success. Successful people oftentimes experience failures. It is almost impossible to have a success story that does not have an element of failure. It may not necessarily be success story all the way. You might need an element of failure sometimes to be able to learn ways that will not work. You must develop an attitude of moving on even when you think you failed in some areas. You must continue to invest what you have to get the desired result. Don't look at the surface; look deep into what is beneath.

Zig Ziglar writes, "*You've only got three choices in life: give up, give in or give it all you've got.*" Life is about the choices we make. Henry Ford writes "*The man who thinks he can and the man who thinks he can't are both right. Which one are you?*" You can fail and give up, you can also fail and get up from where you fell and move on. It's a choice; you decide the option to follow in your life or career.

You can fail today and decide to throw in the proverbial towel and forget trying tomorrow, it's also a choice, but most successful people did not give up when they failed in their first attempt. Persistence is a key element to success. You must continue to fight on. I have closed a lot of sales where it was not expected; where sales were not anticipated. I have also come to a conclusion that making attempts and not making attempts will take the same level of feeling within you. The sequence of attaining a result costs only efforts; it costs only the efforts you will invest in making attempts. If you don't make attempts at all, it also costs the same effort. Someone recently said that staying idle is a big work! Not putting an effort also takes a toll on your energy. It affects your thought process. It takes a lot more energy to avoid a task than engaging in that task. When you are engaged in an assignment, you would be attached to it so much that it becomes part of you and gets easier to undertake. But when you avoid a task, you tend to generate fear inside you which may not be easy to overcome. This is why I believe that it is better to try again when you fail than to stay mute and give up.

It is also a great hindrance not to make a mistake. It is better to try and make a mistake than not try at all. When you try, you learn - even when you didn't achieve what you intended to achieve. Successful people fail more often than average people. They fail more often because they are not afraid to try. They are risk takers, adventurous and enterprising in nature. Successful people believe that success is not served on a platter. But the case is different with average people because they don't try at all; they are afraid not to fail. They are always comfortable with the way things are, and would rather stay mute than take risks.

Average people are too security conscious, they are always in their comfort zones and are always afraid to try or venture into new things. They are so comfortable that they don't want to take risks at all! Taking calculated risks is never in their character. They are comfortable with the average results their comfort zones give them. They are okay with any outcome; they don't happen to things, things always happen to them! Rise up and take your destiny in your hands. When you say yes, the forces of nature will say yes with you, when you try, everything in you will try with you.

In your sales activities, never give up just because your effort today did not yield expected results. Don't assume that the negative result of today will also be the same tomorrow. You can change that negative result by trying again tomorrow. Nothing is constant; the only thing that is constant is change. This is an everyday saying. So believe that the negative result of today must change tomorrow. Believe that the failure today does not result to failure tomorrow; believe also that there is a thin line between success and failure and that thin line is when an individual fails to try.

You learn a lot of lessons when you fail which will position you better not to fail again. Success and failure are sometimes interwoven; they are not distant from each other. What will make you succeed most times is a little shift from the little thing that will make you to fail. A little action or inaction might just be what will make the difference. A medical doctor once said that a patient traveled abroad for medical check-up just because of what he should have corrected with a mere change of life style. The patient was examined and was advised to introduce certain habits and discard some unwanted ones. This was just what the patient needed to get his healing. Success and Failure are sometimes distant cousins!

> *Success and Failure are sometimes distant cousins!*

UNDERSTAND THE BASICS

It takes a lead to develop a prospect. It takes a qualified prospect to discover a customer. It takes a happy customer to discover a promoter. This is a simple sequence in personal selling. The job of the salesperson is to know where to find these leads. As a salesman, the starting point is to ask yourself these questions: what does my products and services do, and who needs them? Use the five Ws and H to unravel the puzzle. When you know what your product is designed to accomplish, it will take you to the next level of finding out who needs it, when he needs it, why he needs it, where he needs it and how he needs it. Leads equal to prospects, and qualifying your prospects takes you to sales. It is true that the more viable prospects you generate the more chances you have to make sales. So the rule is always: make sure you develop enough reliable prospects in your pipeline. Sales takes place when leads are converted to qualified prospects. Ensuring that you have viable prospects at any given time is a necessity in the sales process. This is how to increase the number of customers for your products.

The questions now are: how do you know the right prospect; how do you discover them? Are there prospects that are a waste of time? At what stage do you give up on a prospect? At what stage does a lead become a prospect? Over the years in my sales career, I have come to a conclusion that there are three types of prospects:

[1] The prospects that are viable, they only need follow-up.

[2] The prospects that will never buy from you but will continue to lead you on.

[3] The prospects that will never make a decision to buy; they only bring up objections at every sales call!

As a salesman who wants to succeed, it is not in your place to get rid of any prospect without making sure that he or she is a mere waste of time. I always counsel salesmen not to be in a hurry to discard a prospect unless it becomes obvious that such prospect will end up a waste of resources. This also is the case of dealing with a difficult customer. Some customers are not easy to deal with. They are somewhat fastidious and only bring out the stress in the salesman!

It is always my advice that salespeople should not be in a hurry to thrust aside difficult customers or prospects, unless the salesman has allowed a reasonable time to see if he could manage the situation effectively. When it is proven that it is a tough situation for the salesman to handle alone, he should report the matter to his superiors. It is after following this procedure that apt decisions will be taken. Savvy in Customer Relationship Management is ideal for every salesman. I recommend you take a course in CRM if you have not done so already. In sales, customer is everything.

> *In sales, customer is everything.*

Lead generations, engaging a prospect, qualifying the prospect and customer management are crucial in any sales environment. They make or mar the sales process.

In the art of fishing I talked about earlier, the fisherman does not determine what goes into his net. His duty is to cast his net where he believes there are fishes. He only finds out what is inside later, when the net leaves the water. The net could catch other sea animals or other objects that are not fishes. When this happens, the fisherman separates the unwanted elements from the fishes. This sequence is also adopted by top salespeople. Your duty is to generate the leads and prospects then exclude the ones that are not needed; the ones that would amount to waste of resources. It can be a waste of time, energy and other resources to follow-up a prospect for a very long time without any meaningful result.

It can be frustrating to be following up on the second and the third categories of prospects I talked about earlier. They will not only waste your time, they will waste your physical and mental energy also! The best way to handle this is to determine the sequence of your follow-up that will help minimize the waste of resources.

Let me share this story with you. I once met a prospect during my days as National Sales Manager. He was a wholesale dealer and has a sizeable business outlet. Kelechi, the Area Sales Manager in charge of that sales territory reported the challenges he had been facing in dealing with the prospect. He had been following up on him for six months without any head way. Our man was also not able to secure an appointment for any meaningful meeting with this businessman for this long period of time.

Kelechi reported this matter during our quarterly meeting as a special case, so I decided to get involved in the matter with a view to finding out the category of prospect we were dealing with; so I accompanied Kelechi to his place. When we got there, I observed that the place was quite busy but it seemed the man ran the business with a lone staff - at least I did not see any other staff within the period we stayed there. The setting of his outlet wasn't professionally arranged. The organization of the place could get better; the shelves could be arranged to look more attractive than the way we saw it. The atmosphere looked like a business that has decided that it won't get beyond a certain limit.

In summary, the business needed a little *professional touch*. The place could do better if a little modification and innovation were introduced. The business had reasonable patronage; this could also be leveraged upon to expand the size of existing customers. Remember I went there with the mindset of ascertaining the category of prospect we were transacting with, so observing his environment would help provide the right answer to our quest.

Consequently, Kelechi introduced me to the business owner after we had waited for about five minutes for the businessman to attend to some customers. The owner of the business began with what I would call an *automated response,* saying, "Oga, [which means, Boss in Nigerian Pidgin] you came with him?" He continued, "You see, we don't just want to expand the number of our suppliers, we are guided by our internal policy which allows us to review our vendors every two years," [Note that I did not ask him any question. This was already made shield; inbuilt defense mechanism!] I waited for him to *fire* the first *shot*. When he was through with his opening, I began by greeting him and telling him how great his place was, I waited to see the look on his face which portrayed acceptance to my remarks. I decided to start with that note to enable us a good entry because my intuition had summarized the personality of the prospect already. The best entry would be complimentary.

However, I subtly told him that two years was too long a time to review a list of suppliers because it won't give his business the opportunity to explore other choices in good time. I told him it is better to start reaping the benefits of doing business with us now than wait for two years which is a long time not to reap the benefits our products and services will offer to his business. In addition, I quickly offered him our customer service programme where we assist our customers at no cost in organizing their businesses to be more professional in their services. I didn't want to start talking about our product because I knew that approach would hit the wall; it would be *dead on arrival*! The businessman had raised a policy issue and to continue the discussion successfully, we needed to deal with that first by making him see reasons he should review some standards in his business.

Sales Objections that come from angle of policy is usually sensitive. You need to be very smart to handle such objections. In our case, the best approach was to find a way to buy a piece of the prospect's mind by offering him valuable service at no cost.

I had seen areas that could be improved upon within the period I observed the place; so offering professional services at no cost would have a great effect. I thought in this line because I felt offering a kind of assistance to him should soften his earlier position of not doing business with us. All these were just to start somewhere. We just wanted to see if we could commence the relationship from the angle of giving and investing in his business on customer service basis. We needed to do something that was near abnormal to penetrate the place. Surprisingly, the businessman didn't shift his ground; instead he requested that we give him another three months to think about assisting him at no cost! He said he was traveling on vacation and needed time to think about our offer. I did not want to continue further to avoid spending additional time there; we had spent forty five minutes already. I concluded by thanking him for his time and informed him that the Sales Manager will keep in touch with him. My rule in sales is: Always Leave The Sales Door Open. Just leave it open for tomorrow. The good news could happen tomorrow.

However, Salesmen should note that some prospective customers are like the prospect in the story; they will just lead you on without making up their minds to buy. But in all, you have to stay in charge and be professional. Don't be reactive. Always stay proactive. Don't get irritated because the prospect *wasted* your time without closing the deal. No! This is not allowed in *sales world*. Rather, smile and thank the prospect for his time and promise to keep in touch with him. You will surely keep in touch if the prospect is an ideal prospect, but not the way you previously invested much resources of: time, energy and money. You will have to review the way you visit the place to reduce cost of sales. Business is about inflow and outflow. When expenses are more than income, the business will operate at a loss. When the scenario is incessant, the business will go bankrupt. This is a vital point in sales. The business must stay alive for sales to continue. On the flip side of the divide, sales activities must be effective and efficient for the business to stay alive. The right form of sales keeps the business alive. So there's a thin line between sales success and business success. Experience taught me this.

An ideal salesman is smart, strategic and focused. He takes the best decisions at the right time. He knows when to review his approach. He knows when to reduce the number of times he visits a prospect. You can devise more affordable ways of keeping in touch with prospects if you know they belong to the category of prospects that just lead salesmen on without making buying decisions. You can call them on phone, send them e-mail and periodically pay them visit to see if you can get them to buy. It is advisable that you find a smart way to keep in touch with the market. Giving up is not an attribute of a champion; you must do your best all the time. Success in life is about defining your goals and applying relevant principles that will help you achieve your goals. Always work like a professional no matter the situation.

IT'S JUST A THIN LINE

What differentiates the average person from the great achiever is just a little more effort from the achiever. Athletes often win races with just a slight margin. A second could make someone win an important race in an Olympic tournament. A little effort might just make the difference.

Successful people make things happen. They create the things they want to see, they go the extra mile to get things done. Neil Barringham says *"The Grass is Greener where you water it."* You will notice a change in result in the areas you pay more attention. Salespeople gain or lose sales because of a little action they should have taken more or a little action they took which they shouldn't have taken.

I remember one occasion Maureen and I took our kids Giovanni and Darren to school. It was their second day in school in the new session, so parents were still busy with payment of school fees. It was their early years in primary school. When we got to their school which was located in our estate, Maureen went inside to sign-in the kids, and I waited for her in the car. During that period of waiting, I observed a beautiful woman rushed out from her car with her ward, whom she had brought to school. She had two kids in the car but alighted with one of them. It was obvious that she was in a hurry because she needed to take the other kid to another school. I could see the anxiety on her face. It was about 7.30am, the morning assembly should be commencing in minutes.

This routine should be strenuous for the woman, I thought. As a Salesman, I see sales opportunities in a lot of scenarios. I looked inside her car from where I parked and saw the other child, the expression on his face portrayed that he wished to be with his brother in the same school, so I decided to intervene in the matter.

I didn't need any formal invitation to get involved, I had analyzed the situation. I alighted from my car and waited for the woman to come out from the school. So when she hurried out, I asked her a question in a polite and friendly manner, I asked "Why are the kids not in the same school?" The Proprietor of the school was there watching us; I guessed he heard my question. Some teachers and the proprietor usually come out every morning at the car park to receive the pupils; it's natural that the proprietor's attention would be focused on our discussion because his school was being mentioned in the discussion. When the woman heard my question, she cheerfully turned to me and said that the proprietor couldn't agree with her on the fees. She wanted the two kids to be in the same school but the payment of the fees was not conducive for her and she had to pay for one person, this situation prompted the separation. By the time the woman was explaining this; the proprietor came closer to where we were and joined the discussion. When the owner of the school came to join our conversation, I said to myself that the solution is coming closer. I encouraged the woman to register the other child that morning because the term was still fresh and it was convenient to her for the kids to stay in the same school. It will also make the kids happy. While I was still talking, the woman looked inside her car and observed that her child was listening to our conversation and the look on his face suggested approval.

The situation I created was beginning to yield a desired result! The proprietor seemed interested to shift ground because his body language during the discussion demonstrated that he was willing to concede to the request. The woman was eager to enroll her ward in the school that same morning; apparently she had not registered the other child in the other school for the new session. The child's enthusiasm to join his brother was apparent. So everything was in proper shape to close the *sale* and the owner of the school had to take the long awaited decision. The proprietor accepted to admit the child that morning at a reduced rate, the woman who was visibly overjoyed thanked me for the role I played and took her child inside the school. The proprietor of the school looked at me approvingly and said, "Truly, selling is in your blood!" I narrated the story to Maureen when she joined me. Everybody was happy with the outcome.

The issue shouldn't have waited for my intervention. The matter should have been solved before that time. There is always a thin line between an action and inaction; between success and failure. The difference between the woman's position and the proprietor's standpoint was infinitesimal. The school should have waived it and admitted the second child since his brother was already a pupil in the school. The school should have looked at the benefit of having the entire children of same family in their school which will likely outweigh the reasons of not admitting the second child. There is truly a thin line between success and failure. Business owners should take professional courses in Salesmanship. Today's business is about competence in sales and marketing.

QUIT EXCUSES; MAKE THE CALLS!

I like exceptional results as a salesman; I often remember the period I was recognized as the salesman of the year successively for outstanding performance. I believe that excellent performance is an attitude issue. If you have an attitude of outstanding performance, you will want to keep on with top performance in all you do. Successful people are synonymous with high performance because they want to stay on top. Being exceptional is the only guarantee to staying on top.

> *Attaining success in life follows a given order. You must be willing to climb the staircase to the top.*

Excellence is a great secret to success. Attaining success in life follows a given order. You must be willing to climb the staircase to the top. This is what the school of life taught me. I have also come to the conclusion that one of the things that oppose excellence is excuses. Average people always give one excuse or the other for their failures. They see the toil in every task; they see the *work* in every project. Brian Tracy once said: *"There are thousands of excuses for every failure but never a good reason."* Excuses can't do the job. Excuses won't pay your bills. Get to work!

> *Excuses can't do the job. Excuses won't pay your bills. Get to work!*

I used to work with Ken in my days in the field as Regional Sales Manager; this young man had just joined us barely five months from the time I started coaching him. He was brilliant but his weakness was inability to initiate actions on his own without complaining or giving excuses. He complained about the utility vehicle, the new prospect that didn't smile at him, the environment and marketplace that weren't favourable to him; he gave excuses about the cloudy weather because he wouldn't sell in the rain and so on. He gave excuses about everything!

When I observed this weakness, I made up my mind to assist him. I decided to work on him to be more committed to his job because I believe that when an individual is deficient in this area, a lot of weaknesses will emerge. I worked closely with him for a period of two months. During that period, I made him understood that what makes the difference is the man doing the job and not necessarily his environment. I appraised the outcome of my effort by making him work outside his comfort zone and expecting him to get results. Mentoring plays a big role in changing people's poor attitudes. As a leader, it is your duty to devise strategies that will bring out the best in individuals. This is a vital function of a good leader.

I took the responsibility to bring out the best in Ken. There was a time we got a large order to supply products to a big distributor. The order came shortly before close of work, so we agreed with the customer that it would be delivered to him the following morning. When we came to work the next day, the weather wasn't friendly; it was raining, so I decided to evaluate my coaching period to ascertain if we had made any headway. I told Ken to deliver the order that morning in that rain. I didn't want to tell the customer that we couldn't supply because of the weather; that kind of excuse shouldn't come from Head of Sales and Marketing, who was supposed to be eager to close deals. Delivery time is also a vital issue in selling. The customer might have other business engagements that may require that the order be delivered that morning - so failing in this assignment could affect our business relationship with the distributor.

I had made up my mind that the coaching period was over

and it was time to see the outcome of what he had been taught. This type of situation would have attracted a form of complain from Ken in the past but surprisingly, he assembled the goods, dashed to his vehicle and before I could say *Jack Robinson*, he drove to the customer's place and supplied the products. He delivered the order within a very short time; faster that it would have been if I did the job myself!

Ken seemed to have learned a lot of lessons during those periods of coaching. The approach worked, he stopped giving excuses and his performance improved.

Sales job requires that you deliver exceptional results. No excuses, just expected results! The question now is: How do you get those results? The simple answers are: continue making the sales calls, increase the number of times you meet face to face with prospects and customers, expand your prospects' accounts, have many prospects in your territory and work hard to convert them to customers. Above all, work when you work; don't be caught in the web of unleashing excuses, excuses don't make champions.

I tell salespeople to apply The Selling Champion 10/5/5 Rule of selling. The rule enables effective and efficient sales management. I developed this rule after spending 21 years in the field of sales. The rule is a practical solution to discover, sustain and expand customers. I have taught the strategy in my sales training. It is a smart model in personal selling. Let me explain the rule:

The first instruction in the rule says that the salesperson should ensure that he or she visits 10 ideal prospects daily with a view to starting business relationships with them. The salesman should identify the right prospects in the right market and take the right products and services to them -

with a view to starting a robust business relationship with them. This should be done daily. The target is to reach 10 prospects; not less than 10. If the salesman fails to reach 10 prospects in a day, he should make up the number the next day. This means that the salesman will have to meet more than 10 prospects the next day.

The second instruction in the rule says that the salesman should visit 5 current customers in his sales territory with a view to following up and keeping in touch with them. During this period, the salesman may discover that he needs to replenish stock. It is a good period for the salesman to know how his product is doing. It is also an ideal time to know how the customer and his business are doing. This is a good customer management strategy. Customers are happy when salesmen keep in touch with them. Note also that the target is to visit 5 customers daily. If the salesman reaches less than 5 customers, the same rule in the first instruction will apply.

The third instruction in the rule states that salesmen should visit 5 previous buyers of their products that stopped buying because of one reason or the other. A lot of reasons could make a customer of a company to stop buying products from that company. It could be as a result of competitors' activities, it could be as a result of poor relationship management or reasons that were not addressed. Making this visit will help sort out issues with a view to rekindling the business relationship. My experience in sales profession teaches that it is easier to restart a business relationship that went *sour*, than to commence a new business. The strategy to use here is to find out the reason the "old customer" stopped buying and address it immediately. Explore the healthy relationship that existed earlier and renew the business relationship.

The 10/5/5 rule is a smart sales strategy that takes care of all the segments of selling. It takes care of prospecting and efficient customer relationship management. Today's selling environment is tough and highly competitive. You must devise winning strategies that will make you stand out in the marketplace. The Selling Champion 10/5/5 rule is a smart strategy in the marketplace. Apply it.

Top sales people don't rely on old customers alone. They treat their old customers nicely and move out to secure new sales calls and appointments daily. You must develop new markets daily. Viable prospects and customers are the reason for selling. You must discover the daily.

> *You must develop new markets daily. Viable prospects and customers are the reason for selling.*

Benjamin Franklin said "*The sleeping fox catches no poultry.*" There is no sleeping in sales job. When you sleep, you fail. Sales require steady movement, just like they say in some setting, *No dull moment.* You must be on the move. It is only when you move and make the right calls that outstanding results will come. If you are not active on the job, competitors will take your space. There is no room for poor performance in sales job because what will speak for you are the excellent results you have achieved and not the number of excuses you brought to the table. Excuses don't close a deal on the negotiation table. Quit excuses now and make the difference!

> *Excuses don't close a deal on the negotiation table.*

All dreams are outside of our comfort zone. Leaving that comfort zone is a price we must pay to achieve them. – John C. Maxwell.

SALES TIPS

1. Great things don't happen when you sit down and wait. Go out and happen to things!

2. It takes a casting of net before catching of fishes. Make sure your net or line is always in the water. Move out and seek where the prospects are.

3. The place of determination in selling is irreplaceable. Be determined to succeed, overcome any challenge by your belief.

4. The salesman is a *mobile office*! Don't stop moving; move on and achieve great results.

5. Cast your net where there are fishes. Move strategically, move with precision, and be equipped with the right market information. Strike on target.

6. Sales Job is not an all-comers' affair. You must know the Job, the know-how is not negotiable. Every skill is learnable. Get trained!

7. Be strategic. Where you cast your net is as important as when and how you cast the net. Know your sales environment.

8. Sales Job is like the art of fishing. You need the hook, line and bait. Be prepared!

9. Failure is an integral part of success. When your net does not catch fishes, cast it again! When you prospect and fail the first time, try and try again.

10. The best tool you have is your conviction to succeed. You are the subject; every other thing around you is the object. It takes the subject before the object. It takes you to make things to happen. Be result-oriented.

There's plenty of room at the top but not enough to sit down.
– Zig Ziglar

CHAPTER THREE
ENGAGE TO CONQUER

*People buy for their reason, not yours.
Find out theirs first*
- Jeffrey Gitomer

I teach salesmen to be equipped before embarking on the field. You must know the basics. You must know how to go about the sales job. You must know the sequence of selling. This chapter will look further into the art of prospecting and qualifying your target.

In personal selling, one of your foremost duties is to know your sales environment. You must know the right market, the right prospect; the players in the marketplace and of course relevant information that will help you succeed in your selling. This is how to be strategic in the field of sales. This is the way to do the right things at the right time. This is how to shoot on target. When you fail to understand the market and how it works, you may end up selling the wrong way.

You may have experienced a situation where you spent a reasonable time on someone you thought was a prospect or the right personnel you were supposed to meet? You have done a brilliant introduction and a great presentation in order to impress this fellow and at the end he says something like, "Ok, I have heard all you said, could you come back some other time because my boss who is supposed to attend to you is not on seat!" The dispiriting part is that the fellow will give you all the attention and the impression that will make you believe you were talking to the right person. It is natural that you will release your entire *sales arsenal* while talking with the person. Salesmen are usually not happy when they encounter this type of situation.

The situation can be so frustrating especially for a salesman who is new in the profession. There are some people I call *Notice Me*. These people pretend to be the boss when they are not. They want to receive every salesperson that comes to their place; they want to be seen and noticed even when it's not necessary!

Ijenu, our Corporate Affairs Manager once told me her experience at a marketing consulting firm where she went to meet the Business Development Manager of the firm on a scheduled meeting. We wanted to see how we could collaborate with the firm on a project. The deal started when I met the Managing Consultant of the firm at a conference and after our discussions, we felt we could collaborate with them on the job. The project was a big one and we needed to work in partnership with a firm that shares our vision and values. We also wanted a company with relevant competence to handle such responsibility. We discovered that the firm met our requirements, and we felt we could pull resources together to execute the job; hence we opened up discussions with them.

Ijenu had been discussing on phone with Mr Paul, the Business Development Manager of the firm and they scheduled a lunch meeting to fine-tune positions, though they had never met in person. On the appointed date, Ijenu got to Mr Paul's office a bit earlier before the scheduled time. She met the Front Office Supervisor at Mr Paul's office who took her details and put through a call to the Business Development Unit. Subsequently, Ijenu was directed to the Business Development Department's office lounge to wait for the Manager. She got to the lounge and a well-dressed man walked up to her to inquire who she was. She introduced herself as the Corporate Affairs Manager of our Company and also explained that she was there for a meeting with Mr Paul.

The well-dressed man wasn't in a hurry to introduce himself but was more interested in asking Ijenu what I will regard as nosy questions. As the *drama* went on, Ijenu thought the well-dressed man was Mr Paul or perhaps, a senior official in the company because his disposition looked like that of the boss. So, she maintained her composure and responded to his questions. To her astonishment, another gentleman walked in - when Ijenu was still pondering in her mind about the identity of the person she was talking to and said, "Ben, why are you keeping my guest waiting? Usher her to the meeting room immediately!" And Ben replied, "Ok Sir!" The gentleman then went on to introduce himself to our Corporate Affairs Manager as Mr Paul; he also apologized for keeping her waiting. It was at that time that Ijenu discovered she had been talking to the wrong person for the past six minutes!

It was during her meeting with the Business Development Manager that she got to know that Ben was a newly employed front office staff. The obvious questions would be: What was Ben doing in the Business Development Unit? Was he supposed to interrogate a guest waiting for a manager

- when the Front Office Personnel had got details of the visitor already? Your guess is as good as mine. I call people like Ben, Notice Me. They want to be noticed. They are everywhere. Salespeople meet them every day.

Salespeople experience this situation many times. The question is, what do you do to avert talking to the wrong person, and how do you handle it if you happen to find yourself in such situation? This is why I believe that salesmen should always discover their environment. When you discover, you engage and conquer. You can't conquer what you don't know. Be an expert in what you do. Always try to approach selling from a professional perspective if you want to succeed.

DON'T ASSUME, ASK!

Asking and Listening have been proven to be among the greatest skills in selling and in communication. It is only when you ask that you will know. It is when you seek that you will find. Asking the right question is a great strategy in selling. Asking the right questions gives the salesman direction and saves him a lot of resources. Don't assume you know what the answer is, ask!

In selling, you get a lot done by asking questions and getting responses to your questions. The more you ask questions and listens professionally, the more answers you get on how to handle your prospect. Qualifying your prospect succeeds when you ask the right questions and listen aptly to get the right responses. A lot of salespeople get it wrong at this stage. When you qualify wrongly, you are likely going to sell

> *When you qualify wrongly, you are likely going to sell wrongly.*

wrongly. Asking the right questions and listening attentively for the answers fixes a lot of stuff for the salesman.

In the story, Ijenu should have found out who really Ben was. For example, she could ask, "Did I meet up with our time for the meeting?" And the other person would reply, "Sure you did, you actually came some minutes earlier." This type of reply would of course come from Mr Paul. He wouldn't be able to reply this way if he wasn't Mr Paul. The *wrong person* would be wondering in his mind, which meeting? Ijenu could also say "We have been talking on phone, I am positive our meeting today will conclude the deal, don't you think so? If he wasn't Mr Paul, he would ask "Which phone discussion?" This feedback of course tells that he wasn't the right *guy*.

Selling is not only an art, it is also science. There is the research aspect of selling. You don't just assume things; inquire about things to know the fact and correctness of what you are doing. Ask to know about the new territory you were assigned to. Ask to know about the prospects and customers that will make you succeed in your selling. Ask to confirm if you are talking to the right prospect for your product. Inquire to find out if you are prospecting the right market. Ask to know about relevant industry information. Don't just sell your own way. Ask and get information that will help you sell the way prospects and customers want to buy.

In the previous chapters, I told the story of how the Head of Consumables in a leading FMCG Company gave us marketing research assignment before conducting sales training for them. The earlier information we got before our meeting with the company was for sales training, but the Head of Consumables of the company needed a thorough and all encompassing job and we did the job exactly the way he wanted it. In fact, we exceeded his expectation because he commended my team for doing a great job. Sales is not about what the salesman wants, it is about what the customer wants. Peter Drucker confirms this when he said, "Quality in a service or product is not what you put into it. It is what the client or customer gets out of it." You need to understand this logic as a salesman. Understanding this fact will guide you always.

You need to get to the root of the selling. This is what Conceptual Selling Model teaches. If you understand the concept behind the selling, you will understand how to sell it.

Endeavour to discover the prospect or customer before making your presentation. You need to do this before engaging them. You need to know their likes and dislikes. You need to know their needs and the things that will be solutions to those needs. Buyers buy benefits. It takes discovering them to know the benefits you will sell to them.

Don't assume the prospect you are talking to is qualified to buy your product. Are you sure he is ready to buy and pay within the period you are prospecting or do you think he will buy the product in the nearest future? It depends on what you want to achieve in your selling, unless you are doing product promotion or just creating awareness for you product, otherwise you are supposed to qualify the prospect first before you move on to the next level. Ask questions to bring out his inner motives. The right questions bring out the unsaid and unraveling the unsaid makes the sale.

JUST LEADING ON

I saved our company a reasonable time and resources during Brian Tracy's Seminar Tour in Nigeria some years ago. Our company signed a deal to sell the seminar to corporate organizations and individuals. As a fan of Brian Tracy, we went all the way to get the job done. We already had goodwill existing for us because Brian Tracy had endorsed my book, *The Selling Champion*. People already identify us with the global brand Brian Tracy, so selling the concept was great. We used a lot of strategies to sell the seminar and you will agree with me that good products are the easiest to sell and Brian's trip wasn't different.

I had a *peculiar* experience during the period we sold the Seminar Tour. It was the delay in the decision making of a Managing Director/Chief Executive Officer of an ICT Firm. I had previously discussed the event with the CEO and he invited us for a meeting in his office the subsequent week. I went there with my team and we held what I described as a successful meeting. The outcome of the meeting was hopeful and the CEO agreed that he would get back to us to close the deal when he returns from a trip overseas the following week. Our discussion was hinged on corporate participation at the event which he showed great interest. He wanted to sponsor some of his clients to the seminar as a customer relationship management activity. Subsequently, we waited for his response as agreed but got none. He never communicated either to let us know if there was a new decision or change in plan.

The event date got closer and seats were *running* out as expected, other organizations were keen to fill up the spaces we had reserved for the CEO and his organization but his continuous delay kept us almost in a dilemma. We had promised to reserve the spaces he requested for, so we wanted to play our own part while he played his own. So not communicating after returning from the overseas was an indication that something was wrong. I have been in the sales world for a reasonable time to know the tune of every *sales music!*

Consequently, time kept passing and the CEO still remained mute, so I decided to open up other options. I called my team to brainstorm on the situation and we agreed after our meeting to allow him an additional three days to take a decision or we back out of the deal. Our main concern was keeping our word; we didn't want to disappoint him after promising to reserve seats for his organization. We were also careful not to wait in vain; we wanted to be sure that our waiting was reasonable enough. I teach salesmen to wait when they are dealing with a viable prospect. This category of prospect has the capacity to buy your product or services, or the capacity to refer you to people who will buy from you. I also teach that you find a way to *measure* the waiting period. Waiting for a prospect shouldn't be forever! In sales, you are expected to be *strategically patience.*

Consequently, I decided to call the CEO on phone to ask him a closed-ended question; a question that required a definite answer. So I put through the call and asked a very direct and simple question after exchanging pleasantries, I asked: Do we come tomorrow to seal the deal as we agreed or would you send your representative to us? I listened attentively to observe the tone of his voice. He stammered and said, "I won't be around till next week Monday." "Next week Monday," I asked? Ok, I will call you then, I hung the phone. I wanted to know how the *drama* would end. My instinct had already told me he was indecisive. However, I didn't want to approach the situation as if it was going bad. I wanted to follow the matter to a rational conclusion before exploring other options because there were a lot of options, besides the period we decided to allow for him to take a decision was a reasonable time to conclude with him.

At exactly 10.00am on Monday, the day he said he was coming back, I put through another call, this time he responded and told me he was not yet back. I quickly concluded that the *drama* was over! We decided to move immediately to more viable prospects that were eager and waiting for us. I had told my team earlier to open up discussions with them. The CEO's attitude didn't come as a surprise to me, I had envisaged it. I read a lot of meanings in his inconsistency. My experience in selling guides me to know when to put all my eggs in one basket and when to put them in one hundred baskets! I didn't need any sales consultant to tell me it was time to explore other opportunities. My instinct told me how it would end and I began our Plan B immediately. Successful people are always on the move, seeking alternatives, new ideas and ways of getting things done.

Some prospects will just be leading you on without closing the deal just like the CEO. You need to find out if the person is ready for business or if he is just there to waste your time and make you lose other viable prospects you would have reached out to. Our Plan B worked as expected because we concluded deals with other prospects. We sold off the seats we had reserved for the CEO and his organization in 2 days; just within 48 hours! We would have lost out on both sides if we hadn't taken the swift decision on the matter.

An ideal salesman should observe his prospect closely to know when the prospect is delaying unnecessarily and when he should continue to wait. Some waiting are worth the time while some are not. Some waiting period might just end up aimlessly while some enable the prospect more time to take the right decision. The salesman should find out the type of waiting by engaging the prospects and asking the right questions at the right time. Your waiting should have a direction, not just waiting until you have wasted a lot of time and resources on a prospect. This is what we teach in advanced selling techniques. Successful salesmen are smart people. They take the right actions at the right time.

YOU OPEN WITH THE RIGHT KEY

Have you ever opened a door with the wrong key? I don't think so, if it ever happened, then something must be wrong with the key or the door! We once hired a security staff at our residence. The man was barely two days old on the job and he was learning the essentials. One of the weekdays, I waited some minutes at the gate for him to open the gate for me. After waiting for some minutes, I noticed he had tried opening the gate with more than five different keys until he got the right one. A door can only be opened with the right key, trying to open the door with the wrong key will only upset you. Every key is designed for a particular door. Every door has the right key.

> *Every key is designed for a particular door. Every door has the right key.*

This scenario applies in life too. Life itself follows a process. Life follows a defined order. There are times and seasons of life. Things happen in there due time. There is a time to plant and a time to harvest. It is natural that when you put in the right effort at the right place, you will get the right result. If you understand that life follows a given order, then a lot will be much easier.

I believe that when you know where you are going, any road

will lead you there. When you don't know where you are going, no road will lead you there. This saying applies to sales job too. You need to be precise. Every prospect has a button you need to identify; the button is the key that will open the door of the business you are prospecting. People buy from you when they see that what you are saying makes great sense to them.

I often say that people buy people. Yes, people will buy into what you are proposing if you make them see enough reasons to believe you. Believing in your proposal is a function of performance. Your products and service must be outstanding for prospects and customers to follow you. You must make a mark in the marketplace if you desire a large market share. You must know the way to delight prospects and customers if you want to boost your sales performance. You must earn marketplace loyalty if you truly want to standout.

> *Generic selling strategies don't delight buyers anymore!*

In my book The Selling Champion, I talked about Personalizing Your Selling. You must find a way to connect more with your prospects and customers. The more you connect with them, the more you sell. Today's selling has gone *personal*. Generic approach to selling is no longer ideal in today's marketplace. Generic selling strategies don't delight buyers anymore! Discover your prospects and customers and offer personalized products and services to them. Every good tailor takes the measurement of his customer before sewing clothes for him. You can't sew properly if you don't have the right

> *Every prospect or customer has peculiar needs that require peculiar solutions.*

measurement. This is what happens in the sales world today. Every prospect or customer has peculiar needs that require peculiar solutions. People buy when your products or services can solve their problems. They don't just buy for buying sake. They buy to meet a need. Sell like a champion. Discard generic selling strategies; they are not smart enough. Personalize your selling!

Consider a situation where a banker is prospecting a businessman who wants to expand his business. The best approach for the banker is to present his bank as being able to provide the businessman with the necessary support within the shortest period - if he starts a business relationship with his bank. I call this type of selling: Shooting On Target. In this approach, you identify what the prospect needs and use that as a selling tool. When you identify his needs and the areas he desires assistance, then present yourself as a solution provider. This is vital.

My friend and outstanding banker; who is in charge of sales in a leading commercial bank recently told a story in our masterclass - how he failed to sell to a Governor of a state who happens to be his friend. The seasoned banker had earlier secured a pass for a meeting with the Governor and he went with his team. They wanted to partner the state in a viable project that will benefit the people. What the state needed at that time was affordable housing for civil servants but my friend went to the meeting to sell Advanced Transport System that will improve the Bus Transport in the City. He spent time to explain to the Governor - during his presentation - that the proposed Transport System is the prototype of what is applicable in the city of London. At the end of the banker's presentation, the Governor responded in a friendly tone, "That's a smart idea but what our state needs now is affordable housing for civil servants." The Governor gave his friend a clue that will aid the closing of the sale but the banker was preoccupied with selling the Advanced Transport System. At the end of the meeting, my friend inquired from his team how he performed during the presentation and they all said he sold the wrong product! One of his team members said to him, "Sir, the Governor even gave you a lead that would aid you to change the line of presentation in order to sell what the state actually needed but you kept selling the Transport System!" This is why I promote personalized selling techniques. Personalized selling addresses benefits; it provides solutions to identified needs. Personalized selling strategies follow the concept of Sales Intelligence which enables the salesman to discover the prospect or customer before selling to him. When you discover his needs, you will identify the product or service that will provide solution to the identified needs. This is the way to win in the market.

Prospects don't like stories; let them see what's in it for them. Make them see why they should say yes to your proposal. Once you can do this, the deal is done. Once you are able to identify the right key, the door will surely open.

You can ask to find out what the prospects need at any moment. A prospect can give you a clue if you ask the right question.

You can find out the right key if you know how to get the answers you want. Ask questions and listen attentively for clues. The challenge here is that some salespeople talk too much. They talk so much that they don't have time to listen to decode what the prospect is saying and why he is saying what he is saying. They talk themselves into the sales and out of the sales! Silence is one of the greatest forms of communication. That silent moment the prospect is not saying anything means a lot of communication. It takes a salesman's listening and observing abilities to decode the unsaid words. We will talk more on this later.

The decision making period of the prospect is vital. He thinks through your presentation to be able to make the right decision. Your duty is to make the right presentation that provides the right solution to his needs. Once you find out that the prospect fits into what you are looking for, find out what his needs are and provide solutions. Always come like sales doctor who examines, diagonizes and prescribes solutions. This is the best approach to your prospecting and qualifying assignment. People buy solutions and not products! Show the solution and let the prospect be convinced that your solution fits his situation and the deal is done. Give personalized solutions. This is the key.

> *People buy solutions and not products! Show the solution and let the prospect be convinced that your solution fits his situation and the deal is done.*

JUST LISTEN AND OBSERVE

Charles Anudu, MD/CEO Swift Network Limited, a successful facilities-based telecommunications services provider, once explained in one of our company's conferences where he was a guest speaker that the reason we are created with two ears, two eyes and one mouth is because we are expected to listen twice and observe twice as we speak. This outstanding entrepreneur couldn't be more correct. You need a lot of information to succeed as a salesperson. Listening or observing body language is an ideal selling skills. Listen to understand your prospect and his situation.

When you make your presentation, sit back, listen and observe the body language of your prospect or customer. Just keep quiet, listen and observe to understand him. You only sell when you understand what the buyer wants. You understand what he wants only when you listen.

You will know the next line of action if you understand the prospect better and you do this by listening and observing. Don't assume that you already know what the prospect wants to say. As I explained earlier, silence means a lot of communication. Peter Drucker said *"The most important thing in communication is hearing what is not said."* The prospect is saying a lot when he keeps quiet in your sales conversation. Allow the prospect to let out what is in his mind. You risk a lot when you take over the sales conversation by doing most of the talking without applying the listening and observing skills. Patience is a virtue in selling, it teaches you when to talk and when to keep quiet.

Listening helps you obtain vital information especially when you listen with keen interest. You must listen to understand in order to communicate better. Many salesmen get it wrong in this aspect. Stephen R. Covey says *"Most people do not listen with the intent to understand; they listen with the intent to reply."* I agree with Covey's thought. Many salespeople approach prospects on the premise that they already know what their needs are, therefore assuming there is no need to listen, even when they listen, they interject intermittently. This scenario will not give the salesman the advantage of unraveling the unsaid words. What will make the sale is unscrambling what the prospect is not saying and finding solutions for them. Depending only on what you knew will not close the sale, what will sell is discovering what the customer needs and providing solutions for them.

Be the salesperson who listens to understand before responding. You should understand your prospect's position before replying. It takes understanding before responding, be guided by this simple rule. You respond only to what you understood and you understand by listening attentively.

We should always remember that we have two ears and one mouth. It means we should do more listening than talking. Ask the right questions and listen for a response from the prospect. When you listen attentively, you are better guided to the next level. Stay silent after making a great presentation. You have the same alphabets in Silent and Listen. Figuratively, it means that when you listen, you should also be silent. A good listener stays silent when necessary. Someone who listens attentively communicates and observes carefully too. You can find out or establish a lot when you listen attentively.

Listening attentively is a great attitude in selling and in communication. When you listen to people, it shows a lot of respect. It shows you respect them and you take what they are saying as being vital and you want to hear them out. When you listen conscientiously to your prospect or customer, you establish a good communication zone. You create an atmosphere for cordial interaction. This is also the atmosphere needed to close the sale. You don't close sales when communication is not mutual and effective. Communication is mutual and effective when the two parties are involved in the interaction and not when one party, especially the salesperson monopolizes the sales conversation. Your target should be to achieve a mutual and effective communication and not to monopolize the session you have with the prospect. When you get access to the prospect, make sure you allow him time to express his situation.

Some salespeople get so excited that they have secured access to the prospect and they fail to be guided properly. Getting past the gate keeper is one thing, sticking to the rule of doing the right thing before the prospect is another. You must sell like a professional salesman all the time. Don't be carried away. Take charge of your sales activities and follow the right process.

When you ask questions, let the questions be the type that will help in your customer's business. Always come like someone who wants to help the prospect by trying to identify his needs and finding solutions for them. When you ask your prospects such questions, listen patiently to get the answers you are looking for. The more you ask the right questions and listens attentively to understand the position of the prospect, the more you create chances to sell to him. The right questions create selling opportunities. For instance, you could ask: If I get our management to approve the 2% discount you are asking for, do we supply you the products tomorrow morning? This type of question will likely get a positive response because the salesman is talking like someone who is on the side of the prospect or customer - by making effort to get the 2% discount from his company. Note that the question comes with a commitment. Asking the prospect if you could supply tomorrow morning is the commitment that will close the sale. You could also ask question like: Could you let me know the things we need to do to improve our services to you? This will unravel the unsaid words and help the salesman to explore the world of the prospect or customer. Apt questions create buying atmosphere. Never be in a hurry to sell. Take your time to discover the world of the prospect and prepare an inspiring presentation that will close the sale.

BE A GREAT FRIEND

Human nature is naturally defensive. People are usually apprehensive especially when they meet someone for the first time. Most people you meet in the field the first time as a salesman may not open their hands wide to embrace you. This is natural and it should not bother the salesman. The salesperson is only required to invest all it takes to develop great business relationships with his viable prospects because that's what guarantees sales success.

Conquer every situation in your selling by becoming a friend and a solution provider. Jeffrey Gitomer explained it this way, "*All things being equal, people want to do business with their friends. All things being not equal, people STILL want to do business with their friends.*" When you appear as a friend to the prospect, you tend to bond with him naturally. He frees his mind to do business with you. He exhibits a high sense of trust and both of you will be on the same page to move on.

Aristotle said "*Friendship is a single soul dwelling in two bodies.*" Friendship opens doors for mutual discussion and agreement. It bonds two people together even in business. I always emphasize that it takes mutual agreement before a prospect will say yes to a sale. If there is no agreement between the salesman and the prospect or customer, there won't be any sale. There has to be a meeting point or mutual accord for a sale to occur. This is what happens in an ideal sales scenario. It also takes friendship and mutual understanding to foster this agreement. When you engage the prospect in sales conversation, seek ways that will make the prospect see you as a friend and not as a salesman who wants to make sales. This is a smart way to sell.

It is a fact that people do not like to be sold to, they only want to buy, and they buy from people they like and trust. This trust or likeness takes time to build. It is earned by being consistent in exhibiting admirable character. The salesman earns trust and likeness through summation of commendable attitudes shown to a prospect or customer over the period.

I have practiced this over and over and it has not failed me. I had at one occasion assisted a prospect whose daughter was assaulted by their neighbor. The prospect had received a phone call from his wife about the incident. I was with him when the phone call came through. He was worried after receiving the call and later explained the situation to me. It was a case of assault on his daughter and he needed to report the case to the police station but his vehicle was at the mechanic workshop for repairs at that time. I didn't wait for him to ask me for assistance, I quickly appraised the situation and decided to assist him to the police station since his vehicle was not available and the matter was an urgent one.

Consequently I took him to a nearby police station which was about seven minutes drive from the prospect's office location. We got there, informed the police and an officer was assigned to take care of the situation. The prospect and his wife thanked me for the assistance. What do you think happened thereafter? Your guess is correct! The prospect not only became a customer afterwards, he also became a great friend and a promoter of our products and services.

I could have felt unconcerned and missed an opportunity to

invest in the prospect. I could have missed an opportunity to make a new friend. That period was apt for me to show that I was a solution provider and I took it! Don't be a *straight thinker*. Think also in the perspective of other people around you. Put yourself in their shoes; don't only see your own world, see other people's world too. Show empathy.

The easiest way to connect with a prospect is to make him develop a relaxed mind when dealing with you. You can achieve this by being generous and gracious, just like my role in the story. Giving to people before taking from them shows greatness; successful people always give. Brian Tracy once told us in a seminar that, *"Great people always want to give something. Average people always want to take something."* It is now your duty to decide if you are going to be the salesman who wants to win a prospect by giving or if you want be the salesman who wants to win by taking. In my experience as a salesman, I believe it is easier to go for the former which advocates winning by giving than the latter which is winning by taking. Giving can come in many forms, it can come in your expression of kindness, it can come in your warm smiles and it can also come by giving professional counsel to the prospect in order to make him grow in his business.

THE UPFRONT STRATEGY

Always design a strategy that will set you apart. Successful people are strategic in their actions. We have a strategy we use in our company to maintain and improve our client base for our professional services. I call it the *Upfront Strategy*. This approach seeks to invest in participants that have attended our training. The strategy is simple; we reach out to our corporate clients and extend free advisory services for a period. We also give out free books and offer free mentoring sessions to these individuals. What is the reason for this, what does this strategy do for us? The primary reason for this is to give back to the people who have believed in us over the period. It is a way of saying, "Great friends, we cherish you for believing in us." You know what? Each time we do this; we sustain their patronage and receive referrals from them.

The Upfront Strategy is why we started the first Open Sales Conference in Nigeria tagged: "Nigeria Sales Conference." The conference is the biggest gathering of salespeople in Nigeria. We bring salesmen and other professionals together and build capacity in them. Nigeria Sales Conference hosts top speakers and captains of industry from various sectors in the country. This is our company's way of celebrating salesmen and the "sales community."

My friend who is a certified speaker once asked me how we often get positive response in our seminars and I told him to *Personalize his Selling*. I told him to offer personalized solutions to his clients. The upfront strategy seeks to create a more personal professional relationship with our clients. It is natural to win people to your side when you help them get what they want. Learn how to give free services to your clients. Customer Relationship Management is a broad concept. I promote relational selling. You must find ways to enhance the business relationship. You must find ways to give back to your clients. The grass is greener when you water it. Work hard to build robust relationship with your prospects and customers. Invest in them!

Everything must not be paid for, things that come freely always stand the test of time and they are always remembered. I often talk about investing in the customer and payback period. People will naturally want to pay you back for your good deeds. This is what The Law of Reciprocity supports.

In Social Psychology, **Law of Reciprocity** says that when someone does something nice for you, you will have a deep-rooted psychological urge to do something nice in return. As a matter of fact, you may even reciprocate with a gesture far more generous than their original good deed. Successful salesmen explore the concept of Law of Reciprocity. I believe that the more you give, the more you receive. This is also a Spiritual Law which the Bible expresses in Luke 6:38: "Give and it shall be given to you. A good measure, pressed down, shaken together and running over, for the measure you give, is the measure you will receive. "

When you empower people or show an act of kindness, what you receive is goodness in return. This is only natural. Zig ziglar said, "*You will have everything you want in life if you help a lot of people get what they want.*" Our upfront strategy supports Ziglar's Philosophy. When you give to people, you are expanding your success network. You are expanding your influence zone anytime you invest in people. Sales success requires that you influence a lot of people. The more prospects or customers you influence positively, the more you succeed.

You will succeed in your selling by using this approach. Seek ways to delight the clients you are already serving and you will be sure to generate a lot of reliable prospects from them. This approach has been tested and certified to be workable. This has worked for us over the years. I believe it will work for you too.

LEADERSHIP IS INFLUENCE

One of my best definitions of leadership is the one from John C. Maxwell, "*Leadership is influence.*" This thought from this legendary author can't be wrong. A true leader is appraised by the number of people he is able to influence positively. This follows a simple logic, the more people you influence positively, the more people you lead. People follow what attract them; they are convinced to follow a leader because of what comes out from that leader. The leader influences his people by positive actions.

The world once celebrated the transition of two great African Icons, Nelson Mandela, a.k.a Madiba, and Professor Chinua Achebe. The former was the first elected President of South Africa after the Apartheid regime. He was an epitome of a true and ideal leader that Africa and Africans *exported* to the entire world! He was an exemplary leader who handed over power as President of South Africa after only one tenure in office, even when he spent 27 years in jail for struggles to entrench democracy in his country.

The latter was a literary giant, the *Iroko* of African literature; the master storyteller and author of the internationally celebrated: *Things Fall Apart*, a book written in 1958, which has been translated into more than fifty languages - making him the most translated African writer of all time!

These great Africans were celebrated even in death for distinguishing themselves. It was recorded that over ninety presidents and heads of governments including serving US President at that time Barack Obama and three former US Presidents, George W. Bush, Bill Clinton and Jimmy Carter were in attendance during Nelson Mandela's memorial service! Chinua Achebe was also celebrated by a lot of world leaders both in his country Nigeria, other African countries and beyond. These two African leaders attracted huge commendation even in death because they influenced a lot of people positively during their life time. I celebrate these great Africans.

Leadership is truly influence. When you affect people positively; they naturally become your admirers. This leadership rule also applies in other areas of endeavours, whether in the sales profession or any other career path. You are obviously going to lead as many people as you are able to influence positively. When you empower people or help people to grow, you will naturally have positive influence on those people.

I talk about Brian Tracy anywhere I go not only because he endorsed one of my books, "The Selling Champion." I celebrate this great man because his personal coaching has affected my life and career positively. I see this international brand as a leader who leads and shows the way. We are often influenced by people who affect our lives positively. This is human nature; it's natural. This is why I dedicate this book to him. Brian Tracy is a big factor to what I have become. He is a tool in God's hands. Genuine influence is not bought but earned. Great leaders earn influence by what they do.

Try to give more than you receive. This cannot be overemphasized. The Art of Selling follows this rule also. What will you do to influence the man you are prospecting positively? What will you say differently from what he heard from your competitors that will attract his attention to you? I have said before that sales job is an art and a science. You work with information; you are expected to be equipped with accurate data before you approach any prospect. You are also supposed to have a style peculiar to you that will attract prospects to you.

I have heard a businessman expressed that he likes seeing a particular salesman. He explained that the salesman has a sense of humour which makes him feel good each time the salesman comes around. We all must not be humorous, but we can add something that will make our selling valuable.

A salesperson's appearance or disposition could attract him or her to prospects or customers. Attitude goes a long way in life. Positive attitude is a necessity to success. Maureen and I cherish being attended to by Lawal Modupeola a salesperson at KFC in Ikeja Shopping Mall. Modupeola is simply charming and happy with her job. She smiles all the time. Her smile has the ability to transform an angry person. Her smile is simply *infectious*! She has a way of making customers happy each time she attends to them. You can't help but be on her row waiting happily for her to attend to you. We patiently wait to be served by her any time we visit the Eatery.

During one of our visits to the self-service restaurant, I waited patiently to complete an appraisal card designed by the management of the eatery - where I commended Modupeola for the way she does her work. I don't need to be told that this type of staff will be successful in her career. I wrote this story here to encourage sales folks to find unique ways to connect with people. Be outstanding in your services.

People go to where they are welcomed. People love appreciation and acceptance. Salespeople that have keyed into this secret are the ones that succeed. Sales job is more about the buyer than the salesperson. The prospect or customer is at the centre of the selling. All efforts should be geared towards attracting, sustaining and expanding the customer. The customer is the subject in the sales world the customer is the king! It is your duty as a salesperson to make the customer happy. You can make him happy by your attitude, personality and ability to delight him.

Your appearance and personal grooming is also a factor in delighting the customer. It is often said that the way you dress is the way you will be addressed. I once disqualified a salesperson in an interview because of her appearance and personal grooming. Her personal grooming was not neat and her dressing was not good enough. She however explained that her poor appearance was because she attended the interview in a hurry without having time to organize herself. Her reason wasn't good enough; it wasn't cogent. She failed in one of my sales rules: *People buy you before your product*. She failed to sell herself to us because of her poor appearance. I later counseled her to appear like a professional some other time.

Sales job is a serious business. I tell our clients to hire People Who Can Sell and not People Who Will Sell. You get a good sales team from the period of hiring. You might not get a *perfect salesman* but you could get someone who has the passion and interest in the job that can be trained. Every skill is learnable.

People Who Can Sell in the expression are people with the passion to do the job. They are also willing to learn in order to succeed. The other category: People Who Will Sell are the ones that are not passionate. They just get in to fill-in vacant positions in the sales department! On most occasions, they don't do well in the job and are not willing to learn. They are not willing also to invest in themselves in order to improve because they don't see the necessity in personal and career development. The salesman's attitude and personality are major issue. Know-how can be learned but negative attitude is usually a big challenge. I believe that everything is possible. It is possible to change negative attitude but the fellow must be ready to transform. Changing negative attitude is achieved through mentoring but the fellow must be ready to change.

My ideal salesman is a total package. He is a salesperson that has great self-esteem, savvy in personal selling, customer relationship management abilities, marketing and managerial competence. These are the attributes that attract people to the salesman. This is also why I believe that an ideal salesperson is *self-responsible*.

The salesperson's appearance and his personality could make or mar his selling. Great self-esteem and personal grooming will naturally attract people to the salesman. This stance can get the attention of a prospect. You are not supposed to *dress to kill*, but you are expected to look decent, smart and clean.

Make sure you seek ways to influence the prospect any time you go out for your prospecting. Invent your own style that will win the market! Be creative and unique when you engage a prospect. People are attracted to creativity. Prospects and customers give attention to salesmen who standout. You don't standout in your selling when you lack information about your prospect. You standout and take charge when you are equipped with nuggets of information about where you are going and what you are doing.

> *Do things differently if you desire to achieve different results.*

Do things differently if you desire to achieve different results. To influence your prospect, you should try to know relevant things about the prospective buyer. Try to know your prospect before your first meeting; find out relevant things about him or her. As I explained earlier, this is the function of Sales Intelligence where you employ information gathering as sales strategy. The information you garnered becomes your *Sales Arsenal* when you meet the prospect or customer.

In Sales Intelligence, you find out a lot about the prospective buyer. You discover his kind of person; his personality type, his life style, his social status, what he likes or dislikes. You also discover his buying pattern and the way he thinks. All these help you to sell better. Information is imperative in the art of selling. The more you discover about your target market, the more you devise smarter ways to conquer the market.

When you have adequate knowledge about the person you are prospecting, you build a lot of confidence when you eventually meet him or her - because you will be speaking from a position of strength. When you have done a great job before stepping out, you will achieve positive result. When you do your best in a project, you will likely get the best result. This is a basic success rule. Success in life is not just wished for, it is planned for. If you plan for success and follow the basic principles that lead to success, you will succeed. Success in the sales world follows this Success Rule. Do your best and standout. You have all it takes to succeed as a salesman.

> *To know and not to act is not to know.*
> *– Wang Yang-min.*

SALES TIPS

1. As a salesman, always try to talk to the right person. Be strategic and invest your time wisely. Try to meet the decision maker.

2. Ask relevant questions to unravel what the prospect is not telling you. Be creative and don't probe the prospect. Ask smart questions to get the answers you want.

3. Some prospects will buy your products, while some will not buy. Don't waste time on people who are just leading you on. *Be Sales Wise!*

4. You can't go wrong when you listen twice, observe twice and speak once! Know when to listen and when to keep quiet. Talk only when necessary.

5. Be the friend of the prospect. People buy from friends. People *buy* people.

6. Be *creatively generous* to your customers and prospects. Give free professional services where necessary.

7. Find ways to influence your prospect. Everything works when you get his attention.

8. Do things differently if you desire great results.

9. Research for information. You conquer what you know. The more you know, the more you sell.

10. Be innovative and inspiring in your selling. Be outstandingly different!

We aim above the mark to hit the mark.
– Ralph Waldo Emerson

CHAPTER FOUR
SAILING THROUGH OBJECTIONS

Successful people don't give up. They get up!
Michael Oliver

My former lecturer at the University of Nigeria, J. O. Eneh, Professor of Philosophy, once told us in class that the best way to go through a dilemma is to assume there is none in existence. That class was my first philosophy lecture in the university and I didn't really understand the real meaning of the teaching until I enrolled in the school of life. Sometimes in life, it is better you assume there are no worries, troubles or problems. Just wake up daily, approach the day as planned and do your best to triumph. If you concentrate on your challenges, you achieve nothing! I can now say that I totally agree with my lecturer.

If you approach a tough situation from the standpoint of not seeing the challenge, you are likely going to overcome the stumbling blocks because you didn't see any in existence in the first place. This does not mean that you will be indifferent in the face of a tough situation; it only means you will not allow the challenge to weigh you down.

This thought process of the philosopher has really helped me in many real life situations. I don't see predicaments; I see the opposite side of the situation. I believe that the other side of a taxing situation lays triumph. When you endure and fight on in a presumed demanding task, you will surely overcome. I call this *Winning from within*. Winning from within tells you that you win because you have seen the winning inside you before it materialized. You triumph because you believe you will. What drives you is the victory you perceived from within. What you see is what you get. If you see and think that the mountain is too high to climb, then it becomes that way. If you see the mountain as a *tea party*, then you sip the cup, enjoy it and move on. Life will be for you the way you see it.

Life also teaches that there is no crown without toil. There's always a fight before a victory. You don't just become victorious without a fight. It is after defeating your opponent in a battle that you will be celebrated as being victorious.

These great life lessons are relevant in selling. Sales Objections or Rejections salesmen encounter doesn't mean there is no road. The objection you get from prospects could mean you should try harder. It could signify that you are not asking the right questions. It could mean that you are doing something the wrong way. Objections or rejections might also decide to occur because of internal policy from the prospect or customer or reasons beyond the salesman. Salesmen may not necessarily help some situations. The duty of the salesperson is to keep moving on and keep doing his or her best.

> *If you don't ask the right questions, you may likely get the wrong answer.*

Patricia Fripp once said, "*Life is a series of sales situations, and the answer is No if you don't ask.*" If you don't go for something, you might probably not get it. If you don't ask the right questions, you may likely get the wrong answer. This is the situation life presents most times. Your duty is to be: firm, focused, determined, passionate, prepared and be in control of what you are called to do. These are necessary ingredients to success.

I often counsel salespeople to see sales objection as a normal happening in the world of sales. When you see it this way, then it becomes easy to handle.

Let me ask this question, Do you think a prospect will buy or agree to everything you say without objection? Wait a minute! Put yourself in the prospect's shoes, would you just buy from a salesperson because of the new dress he wore the first day he met you? Or would you buy because the salesperson smiled at you and you found him captivating? These could be good reasons to buy anyway, but most prospects may likely go beyond these reasons.

Nevertheless, some sales objections or rejections could be as a result of the approach of the salesperson. When you don't live up to expectations of the prospects, objections or rejections may be *knocking at your door*. Most prospects would want more logical reasons to buy. They want you to give them more information and details of your product or to educate and tell them more about your products and services. Above all, buyers want the salesman to make them see reasons they should buy his products or services. I don't think you would buy without a good reason. So if you will act in the same way when put in the prospect's shoes, then see objection as a normal event you can handle.

YOU AND THE GATEKEEPER

Prospecting is one of the toughest tasks in sales job. It determines the next step to make in your sales activities. Sales job is the type that takes the salesman to places. Sometimes you are expected to go to places you have not been to - for the first time, you don't only go to these places; you are also required to go and get results.

Most organizations are structured to have offices that will be the point of entry into their premises. You are supposed to go through that entry point before gaining access to such organizations. This is the crux of the matter. If you get this right, you could smile all through, if you get it wrong, you may start counting your losses. Experience has also shown that getting pass the get keeper is one of the reasons folks run away from sales job. I have my fair share of the gatekeeper experience.

Getting past the gatekeeper was one of my toughest tasks in my early years as a salesman. Most organizations I visited, I found out that the gatekeepers would turn to be *obstacles* to gain access to places I was prospecting. The attitudes of gatekeepers could be experienced on phone conversation, e-mail or physical visitation. During my early years in the field as a salesman, I encountered many situations where gate keepers proved to be big issues for me. Sometimes I got irritated and felt like giving up. I didn't understand that gatekeepers were paid to make salespeople like me stay far away from business premises of the organizations - so that I don't encroach in their business time! It took me time to understand that gatekeepers were actually doing their jobs.

Some situations appear more frustrating than others, during that early stage in my sales job. I was in oil and gas industry that period. I remember a particular day I could not hide my frustration in a multinational company. I had visited the company on eight different occasions. Each time I came looking for Mr Fidelis, the Purchasing Manager, I was always asked the same questions at the security post and of course given the same feedback. Questions such as, "Are you on appointment; are you with your proposal? If yes, leave it with us, the appropriate department will get back to you within two weeks." The organization structured their system in a way that you will go through the security department before getting to the front office. I had submitted my proposal to the Purchasing Department through their security department on three different occasions, but they didn't get back to me. The appropriate department never did as they promised and I saw myself coming there eight times without seeing the *right* person! Sales job requires consistent follow-ups. You must learn the art of patience. I have said this several times in this book. You must also do away with anger. Getting angry for your prospect or customer has no place in the world of sales. You must keep your calm and wait for the right time.

My usual character of fighting on helped me a lot. I didn't give up; I told myself that I must devise a way to overcome the issue. Determination is one of the personal attributes I didn't have to learn, I believe I have this character trait in *large quantity*!

Consequently, I went home that day and concluded that I must change my strategy if I truly desire get to Mr Fidelis. One of the approaches I decided to adopt was to involve another party to assist me in the quagmire. I reached out to Chinelo to assist me. She is my in-law who knew Mr Fidelis; they were classmates. I had told myself earlier that I can't continue waiting for, "many" two weeks to pass by without getting a reply from this multinational company. The company was big enough to give me good sales volume that will keep me going while I look out for other buyers.

I was a new salesperson in our company, so I needed results to prove that I was the right man for the job. A good result was what I needed so that my employers won't think hiring me was a mistake. I was determined that the situation I saw at the multinational company must yield positive result. My main challenge was to secure access to the appropriate person in charge of purchases, do my presentation and close the deal. I had lost a lot of time waiting for gatekeepers to give me access; their automated and already made feedback of telling me to come back after two weeks didn't help matters too.

So I told Chinelo my story and asked her to call Mr Fidelis on my behalf because as expected, I didn't have the purchasing manager's personal phone number. The phone number I had was the official one I got from the security department. As requested, Chinelo called her classmate and secured an *executive* pass for me. Her call to Mr Fidelis gave me the opportunity to speak to him the first time after visiting his office eight times. He however explained that he receives a lot of proposals daily and wouldn't have any need to go through them because they already had registered vendors. He also informed me that there was an opportunity to bring in new suppliers since it was the beginning of a new business year. They review their suppliers by that time of the year. I later got an appointment to see him in his office the following day by 11.00am. I didn't have to wait any longer for the automated reply "We will get back to you in two weeks!" I got to their company the next day as scheduled and noticed that Mr

Fidelis had left a message at the security department - indicating he was expecting me by 11.00am. It was truly an executive pass, you would say. I saw the purchasing manager and the rest were success stories!

Now, Let Us Analyze the Situation. I should have known that:

1. The gatekeepers are paid to keep me away.

2. One of the gatekeeper's duties is to make sure he reduces visitors that intrude in their organization's business time.

3. The security department would fail in their duty if they didn't follow their rules.

4. The gatekeepers were not there to stop me from selling; they were only doing their job.

5. I didn't seek a way to build a relationship with any of the gatekeepers. My assumption that they were *obstacles* distanced me from them. This situation didn't help matters.

6. I should have built bridges instead of walls. I should have tried to be friendly with the gatekeepers.

7. If one gatekeeper was a friend, I would have known the company's policy of reviewing vendors annually, which was vital information. Nobody could give me that information because I was *too official*, impatient and didn't see things from the gatekeepers' perspective.

The How:

Tom Hopkins said *"Champions have almost affection for the peskiest objections."* I have come to see objections as a process of success in sales. It's almost a necessity! I often say humorously that "If you sold without objection, you probably sold to your uncle!" My experience today has made me love sales objections; I see them as opportunities to bring out the savvy in me. I take advantage of those objections to prove that I am a master in the *game*.

Develop a mindset that feels that any time you overcome one objection; you get nearer to closing the sale.

Sales objections could be likened to an athlete racing in a long distance contest. Each time he passes an opponent, he gets closer to the last lap, the more opponents he overtakes in the race, the closer and faster he gets to the last stage. The more objections the salesman overcomes, the closer he gets to close the sale.

Don't be afraid to face objections when they come. Never see them as obstacles. If you see them that way, your subconscious mind will send the message to your whole system and your objectives won't be achieved. What made me sail through in the multinational company was the attitude of determination which is innate; this enabled me not to give up on the situation. I may not be seen to have done greatly in handling the situation if I was appraised by the way I went with the security department - the gatekeepers. I should have been friendly and less formal in some cases. Most times, being sociable helps the sale.

> Most times, being sociable helps the sale.

The situation I encountered would have been easier for me if I had tried to be a friend to the personnel at security department and not a salesman who wanted to gain access in a multinational company. Finding a way to develop a cordial relationship with the men at the security department would have allowed me access to some vital or privileged information; at least somebody should have informed me the company review list of suppliers annually. When you see objections as a time to prove your worth then it becomes easy to handle. Attitude is everything. I can't agree less with this thought.

Any time you sail through one barrier of sales objection, you step up to another level of sales opportunity. Stop seeing objections; see them as opportunities to tell more about your products or services. It could be that the situation wants you to be more patient or to be more professional. Sales objections could also be an opportunity to prove that you are a Sales Superstar as Brian Tracy would put it. Take that chance and close the sale.

> *Any time you sail through one barrier of sales objection, you step up to another level of sales opportunity.*

NOBODY IS LESS IMPORTANT

In the Sales World, everybody is important; no matter what you think. The human body explains it better. The body needs the eyes for seeing and the legs for walking. You need the mouth for speaking and the teeth for chewing, and so on. Just as it is in the human body, so it is in sales job, every man or woman in any organization you are prospecting, or you are selling to already is important to you as a salesman, no matter his or her position. You need people to succeed at any given time.

My friend, who supplies security gadgets and one of the biggest suppliers of surveillance equipments in Lagos, told me a story about a company he does business with. He said that his contact person in that company was the Managing Director, MD. He comes there at the instance of the MD and gets things done through that contact. However, he devised a way to be friendly to other employees of the company even when the MD was his ally. He developed a friendly relationship with the Deputy Managing Director, DMD, whom he addressed as *the boss*. Each time he was around the premises to see the MD for one business or the other; he would see the DMD in his office before seeing the MD.

My friend continued his supplies there for a period of four years without any hitch and maintained robust relationship with the Deputy Managing Director. Then the twist came! The MD, my friend's close friend was retired from the company because he had served his tenure of five years as the Managing Director and had reached the retirement age of the company. The mantle of leadership now rested on the Deputy Managing Director. The New Managing Director took over formerly and reviewed the list of all their suppliers and behold, my friend's company was retained. Guess what? The supplies continued in an incremental rate! The boss that was imagined later turned out to become the real boss! In sales job, everybody is important.

Sales job is the kind of job where you need to develop cordial relationships with everyone. This great relationship should be extended to the personnel in the cleaning department who clean the offices of the high and the low in the organization. You need to extend this friendly relationship to the office attendant who sends out files from one point to the other and runs other errands for the company you are prospecting or the one you are already doing business with. You need cordial relationships with the accounts department's staff at least to ensure that your payment file doesn't get "stuck in transit!" In sales, you need to know all the people who matter and the ones you think don't matter.

This is what makes you sail through objections easier in organizations. When you develop cordial relationships with staff of any organization you are doing business with or the ones you intend to do business with, you will notice that the people who will be for you will outweigh those who will be against you. This is one of the strategies you need to get your selling right in order to achieve sales success. You might know the fundamentals of the sales process and not get it right in this area. It is one thing to get the basics right, it is another to make the environment work for you. Advanced selling skills require that you develop this kind of atmosphere. This is one of the attributes of The Selling Champions, which are learnable and doable. This is a strategy we have practiced overtime and I can tell you that it works.

> *In sales, you need to know all the people who matter and the ones you think don't matter.*

THE PHONE SUCCESS

Securing sales appointments over the telephone is an area many salesmen encounter a lot of hurdles - especially if they are speaking to a prospect for the first time. It could be to introduce their company or to secure an appointment or for any other official reasons.

Cold calling is the sales process of approaching prospective customers or clients via telephone, email or social network who was not expecting such interaction. Cold calling is not popular in some parts of the world though it's very common in some economies.

In some countries, prospects would prefer to see the salesperson in person while in other clans; this might not be the case. Sales activities can take place face to face or over the phone.

However, no matter which side of the divide you operate from as a salesman, you might require initiating transactions via telephone from time to time. It could be that you want to secure a sales appointment, or tell the prospect about your products and services, or that you want to say one thing or the other about your company. As a salesperson, you may have discovered a lead from a catalog, the Internet or any other source and think it would be a great idea to put through a call to close a deal or book sales appointment with that contact.

This does not always come as easy as it sounds. Getting through phone calls oftentimes is a hard *nut to crack*. A telephone conversation to a prospective customer is a serious issue. Before you encounter any objection from the receiver or prospect, make sure your *house* is in order. You need to give the telephone call every attention it requires. Organize yourself, get your writing materials and be at your best. Remember the prospect is not seeing how beautiful you look or how gorgeously dressed you are, what will attract his interest is how you sell yourself on the phone. The more apt, appealing or interesting you sound, the easier and faster the prospect buys into your proposal.

Let's look at these samples of phone calls from two salesmen in a consulting firm to a prospect:

Salesman A: "Hello Mr Prospect, this is David from ABC Consulting Company. I'm calling to introduce you to our new training programme for salespeople. There are many ways the programme would be of benefit to you."

Prospect: "I believe this is your number; we will get back to you." Or the prospect might say: "We already have an in-house Trainer for our salespeople, thanks for your interest in us!"

The prospect David made this call to would have been so magnanimous not to hang the phone on him! You can't tell a prospect who doesn't have all the time in the world "There are many ways the training programme would be of benefit to you!" Most prospects won't get back to the salesman as they promised because the call was not inspiring enough. Telling David about having an in-house trainer might be a polite way to discard his proposal. The chapter two of this book talks about the line, hook and bait in the art of fishing. It takes the bait to catch a fish. An ideal call will have a hook that would get the receiver's attention. The salesman needs to add "flavour" and creativity to the phone call. Consider this approach:

Salesman B: "Hello Mr Prospect, this is Zara from, The Selling Champion Consulting Limited."

The salesman would say in an inspiring manner: "I'm calling to book an appointment with you to discuss a new strategy we just developed that will help your salespeople shoot their sales figure up by 30%!"

Prospect: "Shoot our sales figure by 30%?"

Salesman: "Yes, we developed a unique model that we will share with your team; can we schedule to meet on Tuesday at

10.00am in your office?"

Prospect: "In my office? Okay! Let's see on Tuesday at 10.00am."

Who does not want to increase his sales figure? People love good news, give it to them!

Salesman B will likely get the deal because his approach is inviting and backed up with benefit.

Salesmen make or mar their sales activities on phone because of lack of preparedness or not being creative enough. Business people don't manufacture time! They don't have the spare time to listen to a salesman who is not inspiring enough or who doesn't have the ingenuity to keep them long enough on the phone. When the salesperson sounds uninteresting on phone, the feedback he or she will likely get is objection or rejection. Inspire your prospects!

THE DIGITAL WORLD

Digital Sales and Marketing is the way to go today. With the emergence of search engines, content marketing, data-driven marketing, e-mail direct marketing and social media marketing; the digital sales and marketing environment has become a vital aspect of business. Facebook, Twitter, WhatsApp, YouTube, Linkedin, Instagram, etc have made great marks in the digital space; organizations utilize these platforms for marketing purposes.

The digital world provides sales and marketing professionals broad opportunity to sell or position their products and services. Our company utilizes this platform in many ways but you must develop competence in this area - if you truly want to take advantage of the digital space. You must know how to develop contents and how to create followership in the digital marketplace. You must choose ideal audience and supply them with the right information. This is the way to build followership in digital sales and marketing. You can also experience sales objections in this area if you don't know how to go about it.

Let me talk about electronic mail which is a part of digital tool; which is often utilized for official messages. Messages you send to your prospect or customer via this means must have valuable content. Many people won't bother to go through mails that are not attractive enough. The content you put in your email is important. The way you communicate the content is very important. This is the main reason electronic mail fails or succeeds.

I know you may have received electronic e-mail before and you didn't bother to go through the details. I have done this on several occasions! Most times I don't bother wasting time on certain messages. I see some of such mails as sheer waste of time. E-mails from salesmen could suffer these kinds of objections or rejections if the sender fails to follow simple procedures that will make his messages attractive enough to the receiver.

Utilizing electronic mail is an important aspect of sales and marketing. Proposals and various sales communications are sent through this means. However, I don't usually advocate that sales professionals should use e-mail as the only medium for their sales communication. The electronic message should not replace face- to- face sales conversation especially when you are yet to convert the prospect to a customer. Nevertheless, e-mail could be used as a supplementary effort or where the salesman is finding it difficult to sail through the gatekeeper.

When the e-mails fail to go through, the salesman is usually dispirited. Sometimes, salesmen don't receive reply for proposals. It is quite challenging when this is the case, because, just as it is in telephony, so it is also in electronic messages; you don't see the face of the receiver of your message. The solution is that the salesman reviews his approach. The salesman's style of communication via the electronic mail matters a lot. It is ideal that your message is interesting, important, precise, short and simple; even when the receiver is not seeing your face.

The receiver might decide to ignore your message because it doesn't simply appeal to him. The receiver might even decide to reply with an objection that will throw the salesman off balance. In the media world, we were taught to keep it short and simple "KISS." Let the message be concise and apt. Unnecessary lengthy messages may give rise to objections or rejections. Prospects may raise *stumbling blocks* so that the salesmen will let them be!

In structuring your e-mail, ensure that the receiver reads the *big story* first. After your friendly greeting and gripping introduction, let the compelling message you want to pass across follow immediately. Don't save it for the last. Let the most important part of the message come first. Most online prospects or customers are impatient to read through to the last paragraph of your message, which probably includes what would attract their interest. Tell the big story first! This is what will sustain

> *If you don't catch the prospect's attention from the beginning, you may not grasp it subsequently and what you get consequently is objection.*

the tempo of the reading. If you don't catch the prospect's attention from the beginning, you may not grasp it subsequently and what you get consequently is objection. Introduce the HOOK within the first paragraph!

Ensure also that you state clearly a feedback medium. Make available your contacts, a functional website, phone number, office address and other relevant information that will aid in reaching you. One of the aims of electronic mail is to secure appointment with the prospect for your sales presentation. If you are lucky to close a deal via your first message to a prospect, then you are one of the luckiest salespeople but in most cases, the best you can get is to book an appointment with the prospect for a face-to-face meeting.

Always remember not to be in a hurry to send out messages without reading through again and again. Most people may not be in a hurry to read e-mail that is not presented properly. Read through, edit and make corrections where necessary. Don't rush in only to rush out! Be inventive in creating the message because the prospect is not there with you. The thing that will sell the message is the magnetic power which is shown in your ability to communicate aptly the value you want to transfer to the prospect. Prospects will likely spend few moments or minutes to go through a well articulated electronic message. Make yours one of those!

OH! THE PRICE IS TOO HIGH!

We once carried out a survey within a group of One Hundred Middle Class Professionals to find out the reason people buy with regard to price and quality. We wanted to find out if people attach more importance to price of the product or quality of the product. The feedback we got from the survey read thus:

40% of the respondents prefer good quality products without considering much about the price.

54% desire good quality products at affordable price.

2% have a preference for lower price without minding the quality of the product.

We allowed 4% as margin of error.

The above simply testifies to the fact that people want good quality and great value, though more people want good quality of the product to go along with affordable price. Peter Drucker's expression that, *"Value of the Product is not what you put in it but what the Customer gets out of it,"* couldn't be more correct. The question now is: How do you make the Customer or prospect see the quality in your product?

In our sales masterclass, we teach that the value in a product is not only in the product you are giving to the buyer. The value is in the total offering the customer is receiving. The value is in the benefits in the product. The value is in the salesman's ability to present his product and services convincingly to the prospect. The value is in the creative style of the salesman. The value is in the self-confidence the salesman exhibits when he talks about his product. The value is the salesman's ability to love his product and transfer the feeling to the prospect. Great value is when the salesperson is able to convince the buyer that he is paying less for more. Above all, the value is in the great quality of the product.

When the salesperson faces this hurdle of *the price is too high,* the best way out of this type of objection is to highlight the

> *The main duty of sales presentation is to show the features, advantages and benefits of the products and services in such a way that the prospect or customer will feel he is getting more value for little money!*

quality of the product. In Nigerian Pidgin, we say, "Beta Soup Na Money Make Am." Good soup will naturally require more money to cook. Let the buyer or prospect see that he is actually getting more value if he pays the price you asked him to pay. If you are able to make a case that the worth of your product is more than the price you are selling it, the price objection will be solved. This is the main focus of the salesman during sales presentation. The main duty of sales presentation is to show the features, advantages and benefits of the products and services in such a way that the prospect or customer will feel he is getting more value for little money!

Let me tell you my recent experience on the issue of price. When I launched my book, *The 25 Unbreakable Laws of Sales* that became a bestseller, I wanted a book that will stand out in the bookshelf. I told myself that if I wanted a book of this nature, I must go the extra mile to make it happen. Then the journey began. It took me three years to write the 520 page book. After I concluded the writing, I reached out for notable endorsements that will make the book unique and I got 11 of them! The book became the most endorsed and most voluminous book on practical selling in Nigeria! Leading captains of industry, corporate experts and academics read the manuscript and endorsed the book. The content of the book was outstandingly inventive, enlightening and thought-provoking. The packaging was hard cover. The paper type was "off white" colour. The cover design was captivating, and the font size was readable and friendly to the eyes. We unveiled the book, distributed it to notable bookshops and fixed the selling price that is reasonably affordable. Many professionals and business people bought the book because of the value and some prospects felt the price was expensive at N5, 000 a copy. While the book was doing extremely well in the market, we also got feedback that some prospects wanted reduced price.

As a marketing professional, I began to cultivate the thought of publishing a different category of the book for another segment of the market that will be more affordable. I like to consult a lot when I want to take vital decisions. I went to my good friend, Kachi Onubogu, outstanding marketing professional and a *big player* in the multinational environment. Kachi was at the book launch and he followed the chronological events concerning the book. He once commended me about the book and informed that he makes reference to the book when training his sales and marketing team.

So on that fateful day, I went to Kachi to seek his input on publishing a reduced price version of the book for students, trainees in sales job and starters in the corporate environment. But Kachi wasn't convinced with my plan. He wondered why anyone - who wanted value won't buy the book at the selling price of N5, 000. He felt the price of the book was appropriate. This is a true case of where high quality took care of price objection.

In my experience in my professional life, I believe in excellence. I believe in good quality. We always go for the best in everything we do in our company. We make sure our products and services maintain high quality. This is why we utilize high profile speakers in our masterclass. We believe that high quality kills price objection. The more you distinguish yourself by offering high quality products and services, the more you weaken sales objections. This is what I have come to believe overtime.

> *The more you distinguish yourself by offering high quality products and services, the more you weaken sales objections.*

It has been proved earlier that people want value. I have not seen where people go out seeking to buy inferior products. People want to buy good quality; they want the best products and services. They want to get value for their money.

The salesman could also use after sales service if his company allows such as incentive for his prospect to buy. All these could be summed up as total value of the product. The concept of price and cost in selling is broad. The buyer's cost of the product includes the toils expended before acquiring the product, while price is the price tag on the product. When the buyer sees that he is getting more value than the cost of acquiring the product, he is likely going to buy, when the reverse is the case, then the challenge of price objection will arise. It is the duty of the salesperson to show the prospect the value during his presentation. When this is achieved, price objection will likely be defeated.

Another way to handle objections is to answer the objections yourself before going to the prospect. Create a scenario where your team x-rays and addresses possible objections before visiting the prospect. When you identify possible objections, answer them before reaching the prospect or customer.

Answering objections before engaging the prospect is a strategy I often recommend for salesmen because it has the capacity to handle the extensive scope of sales objection.

Before you meet your next prospect or customer, look at the likely issues the buyer might raise and answer them yourself. This strategy puts the salesman in charge of the sales conversation because what is expected is usually averted.

THE WORLD OF REJECTION

I always recommend that salesmen stay positive whenever they encounter any form of stumbling block. It doesn't matter if it's coming as an objection or a rejection; what matters is that the salesperson should remain focused, undaunted and impervious. The attitude of never giving up and developing a *thick skin* should be the strength and motivation of the salesperson who encounters any form of rejection. I often advise salespeople to try and try again in the face of rejections until it is obvious that they should move on.

Objection or Rejection is a necessity in the ladder of success in the sales world. The salesperson may not develop in his career if all sales came on a platter. The challenges salespeople encounter help to develop the man making the sales. He learns from his mistakes, improves and launches back as a better person.

However, some rejections or objections might not be the fault of the salesperson. The salesman may have tried all he could to close a deal but still failed. The prospect or buyer may raise issues that will disqualify the salesman from the sale. It could be a policy or internal issues originating from the prospect's company, or things the salesman doesn't have control over. I call them, Real Objections. You can't do much to change the situation when they want to emanate. When this is the case, the salesman should not stop exploring other opportunities. He should move on with the right mindset until he achieves his target.

Even the best and global celebrities have experienced rejections at one time or the other in their careers. Let's share some examples culled from Jack Canfield's work:

The examples I am going to share with you were told by the Celebrities as testimonials. It should be an inspiration to anyone who is encountering any form of rejection. I believe they will motivate you.

Here's a copy of the reply by the President of a recording company to Madonna the pop star.

The letter reads:

Mr Alec Head
C/O Media Sound
311 West 57th Street
New York, N.Y. 10019

Re: MADONNA

I enjoyed listening to Madonna. The production, arrangements and she are very strong. The direction is good one, in my opinion. The only thing missing from this project is the material. I liked "I Want You," "Get Up" and "High Society," but I did not like "Love On The Run" at all. I do not feel that she is ready yet, but I do hear the basis for a strong artist. I will pass for now, but I will wait for more.

Good luck and thank you for thinking of me.

Best regards
Jimmy Lenner
President

Note: when the Queen of Pop finally signed with Sire Records in 1982, her debut album sold more than 10 million copies worldwide. She used this early rejection as motivation as this respected producer didn't believe she was "ready yet." She's now the best selling female artist of all time.

RSO Records [U.K] Limited
67 Brook Street London WIY IYE England
Cables Stigwood London WI
Telex 264267
Mr. P. Hewson
10 Cobewood Road
Dublin 11
10th May, 1979

Dear Mr Hewson

Thank you for submitting your tape of [U2] to RSO, we have listened with careful consideration but feel it is not suitable for us at present.

We wish you luck with your future career.

Yours Sincerely

Alexander Sinclair

Note: When U2 debunked in 1979, RSO Records was thoroughly unimpressed. Within months, the band signed with Island Records and released their first international single, "11 O' Clock Tick Tock." They went on to sell 150 million records, win 22 Grammy Awards [most of any band ever] and performed in the highest grossing concert tour in history.

Let's look at other famous people and the rejections they encountered:

Opray Winfrey Fired as an evening news reporter of Baltimore's WJZ TV because she couldn't separate her emotion from her stories.

Walt Disney Fired from the Kansas City Star in 1919 because he "lacked imagination and had no good ideas."

JK Rowling Rejected by dozens including HarperCollins, when a small publisher in London took a chance on Harry Porter.

Steve Jobs Fired from the company he started, Apple, but was desperately brought back in 1997 to save it. Apple is now the most valuable company in the world.

Abraham Lincoln Demoted from Captain to Private during war, failed as a businessman and lost several times as a political candidate before becoming president. The list is limitless.

I have experienced my share of rejection. One of my family friends who once operated a business development company didn't believe that our company has the capacity to train his company's personnel. I had approached him to give us sales training jobs but he told me that we lacked the capacity to train his staff. He also didn't believe that training has any positive effect on performance. His company has over 2, 000 salespeople at that time but my friend felt his business model was unique and there was no need for capacity development. I made several efforts to convince him but his position on the matter was firm and I left, feeling disappointed. But somehow, I moved on. I decided to see the experience as a motivation instead of rejection. Though the business development company later crumbled because of regulation issues but lessons were learned.

Today, our company has made an outstanding mark in our industry. We have won distinguished awards! The greatest form of objection or rejection is the one that comes from you.

> *The greatest form of objection or rejection is the one that comes from you. No man can stop you except you. If you doubt yourself, then you are courting failure.*

No man can stop you except you. If you doubt yourself, then you are courting failure. Never accept negative scripts written by naysayers. Move on with your great dreams and win your battles.

A lot of successful people have stories that are quite motivational. I always advise that you develop the right mindset that will encourage you to move on even when the environment says NO to YOU. Create the right big picture in your mind - which is your vision. Believe in that big picture and work hard to achieve your dreams. When you follow this success sequence, objection or rejection won't be an issue because you know where you are going and how to get there. No amount of challenges can stop You!

The people who went on to tell their inspiring stories believed in their dreams, they saw what the people who appraised them didn't see! They saw possibilities when others could only see impossibilities and limitations.

Salespeople should learn from this. Objections and Rejections may likely occur once you want to exchange value; once you want to sell something. Buyers want to be sure of what they are buying. They want the best deal that is why they bring up objections or rejections. The responsibility of the salesperson is to prove to the buyer that his offer is the best. The salesman should also develop the right attitude that will motivate him during the period of rejection. The right attitude will surely give the right direction.

It always seems impossible until it's done. – Nelson Mandela

SALES TIPS

1. Sales objection or rejection is not a prison sentence, it's part of the *game*!

2. Always believe that when you sail through an objection, you get nearer to closing the sale.

3. If you sold without objection, you probably sold to your uncle!

4. You can win from within; you can also lose from within. It's your call, be positive.

5. To the salesman who is prospecting an organization, everyone is important. The boss is important, the office assistant is also important.

6. The more people the salesman wins to his side, the lesser objections he encounters.

7. Start building bridges now; break every wall!

8. Sales objection could mean interest in disguise. Be guided by this thought.

9. When you make sales calls, sound convincing. When you send electronic messages, keep it short and simple.

10. Impatience is not one of the virtues in the world of selling. In Sales, Patience is a Virtue.

It is not in the stars to hold our destiny but in ourselves.
— *William Shakespeare*

CHAPTER FIVE
MAKE THE SALES

Nothing happens until a sale is made.
- Red Motley

One way to achieve results is to perform greatly. You need to invest effort in order to get things done. The amount of work you put in a project will naturally determine the level of your achievement in that project. You are expected to move on to the last stage if it's what is required to accomplish an assignment. No matter the obstacles you experience in trying to accomplish your goals, you are expected to hang on until you come out victorious.

Nothing good comes easy, greatness does not come effortlessly; and it comes with a price. Success comes to the people who desire it and are willing to go the miles it takes to get to the top. It is always advisable to try and try in any laudable task until you succeed. Don't be afraid to fail in a project, let your motivation be the result you want to achieve in that project, when you think and act this way, you get closer to your success story. It is better you try to achieve a result and fail than not try at all. When you try and fail, you learn ways that will not work and move on. When you don't try at all, you learn nothing and will stagnate where you are.

Don't be discouraged because you are afraid to fail. Do your best in your job with required vigour and commitment and believe you will succeed.

Your goal in going through the sales process of: lead generation, prospecting and qualifying your prospect; developing cordial relationship with the prospect and identifying his needs, making your presentation and handling possible objections that may arise and asking for the order, is to make a sale. Every effort you make should lead to a definite direction. You must identify your reasons for selling. You are not in the field of sales as a salesman for nothing. You are there for a purpose. Experience has taught me that three major assignments that await the salesman each time he encounters a prospect or customer are to:

1. Make a sale that will provide a solution to the buyer.
2. Open and sustain a cordial relationship with the prospect or customer.
3. Devise smart ways to expand the number of people who buys his products and services.

Closing a sale is a serious business in a sales job. It is a major factor in selling. Closing sales is one of the main reasons for the salesman's toils. The salesman is happy when he closes a sale or opens a relationship that will yield positive results in future. We cannot over emphasize the importance of what closing a sale means to the salesman. It is one of the main reasons salespeople apply all the strategies they use in trying to woo the prospect. It is why you are expected to be at your best before seeing a prospect.

Closing sales does not just happen; it is planned. You plan for it to happen. Unless it is a situation where customers walk into your business premises in an open market situation to buy from you, such customers may have known about the product through marketing activities, otherwise every sale in personal selling situation is calculated.

In an ideal personal selling situation as explained previously, you are expected to follow up a prospect from lead generation phase to the stage where you make the sale. You are expected to succeed in all these stages because in the sales world, everyone talks about top performance. Always prove your worth in the field of sales. Folks will celebrate you when you distinguish yourself. Keep Selling!

THE LAW OF ONE MORE TIME

In the course of my career which started as a salesman and subsequently to a sales and marketing consultant, certified trainer, bestselling author, speaker and high performance coach, I developed a strategy I call "The Law of One More Time." I used The Law of One More Time to close a lot of sales during my time in the field. The Law of One More Time tells you to try one more time before you give up on a deal, on a prospect or customer, or before you close for the day.

I use this strategy to keep on engaging prospects and not giving up so easily. Closing sales does not happen quickly most of the times. It takes its own time and pattern to happen, but it is expected that the salesman navigates this pattern and time to a desired expectation.

The Law of One More Time tells you to dial the phone number one more time when the prospect is not answering your calls. This law encourages you to see the presumed tough prospect again or to move on to the next prospect one more time - either to seek an appointment or to make your presentation before you close for the day. The Law of One More Time tells you to try again one more time in those things you failed to achieve previously. I have also come to notice over the years that most times you try again one more time, you achieve the unexpected.

Closing sales should be planned strategically. Take your time to plan the beginning and the ending of the process. This law of one more time will encourage you to move on when you want to give up because of objection or any other reason. The Law of One More Time will encourage you to hang on when you have discovered a reliable prospect; it tells you to wait for the prospect patiently to take his decision.

Average people don't like undergoing any form of pressure. Most people like *already made*; they prefer tables that are set! They wouldn't like to work their way to the top but want to get to the top. It is ideal to develop a mechanism that will propel you to action. This inbuilt mechanism of *The Law of One More Time* reminds you to work hard all the time. It *fuels* your energy to move on even when you want to give up on an assignment. It is when you don't give up on a prospect that you will finally succeed in converting him to be your customer.

Some salespeople give up at the slightest attempt. They give up when they visit a place twice or more without getting order to supply. They also conclude easily after few visits that the prospect won't buy from them. This quick decision making is not advisable in selling. It is ideal that you follow through your prospect to a logical conclusion. You will know the ones who did not buy because you didn't do enough and the ones that won't buy even if you *submit your grandmother's birth certificate!*

The Law of One More Time is a great guide for the salesman. Always encourage yourself to try one more time when you are not getting the desired result. You will know the right time to give up on a prospect and the time to continue to try. Your duty is to work hard towards the right direction. Have the right attitude to work and believe in your abilities to achieve your goals. When you do this, all the possibilities you envisaged will fall in place.

THE MORE THE BETTER

I recently spoke to a group of 400 men in a leadership summit, I spoke on the topic: Influence: the Power of a Leader. I told the audience that the more you invest in people or add value to their lives, the more you expand your influence zone. This is the way to build a great legacy. American poet and civil rights activist, Maya Angelou once said, "Your Legacy is the lives you touch." I agree with this great mind.

> *Genuine Influence is when people willingly follow you because of you and not because of what you have. Genuine Influence is given and not taken.*

The more you bring happiness in your environment, the more you smile. This is natural, I believe. This philosophy goes further to posit that if you help ten people realize their dreams, you have created ten friends; you have discovered ten new people who will be on your side.

The more you affect more people positively, the more you increase your influence on them. I call it *Genuine Influence*. Sometimes, influence is coaxed and not earned. Genuine Influence is when people willingly follow you because of you and not because of what you have. Genuine Influence is given and not taken. Maybe, we will talk more of this in my leadership book, watch out! But in all, it is ideal that you do your best by your character, attitudes and actions to win people to your side.

The sales world is an environment where number counts. The amount of sales you make is important. The amount of money you bring in through sales is vital. These must be on the increase all the time because they are the lifeblood of every organization. This is where genuine influence comes in. It is to the salesman's advantage to have a lot of people on his side. It is to the salesperson's interest to have a lot of viable prospects and customers on his list. The more qualified and happy prospects you have on your side, the more chances you have to make more sales. You sell to people, you can't sell when you dwell only on imagination, you sell when you imagine and go out there to make those things you imagined to happen. Go out and make more qualified prospects that will become customers!

Selling is a practical thing, it is an active job; it doesn't believe only in rhetoric. You talk and act; you are expected to walk the talk. You say it and do it; you must show results. You must take relevant action. You are either selling or not. You can't be a selling champion in a day, but you must be seen to be improving in your daily sales activities. Working hard ensures improvement in performance. The harder you work, the luckier you will be! This thought can't be overemphasized.

Success is found when you are uncomfortable with being comfortable. Create discomfort around you! What guarantees success most times is doing things that will give you discomfort. Work extra hours, visit more contacts, talk to more people, engage in more activities, wake up early, and do more creative thinking. These processes belong to the man who likes discomfort; they belong to the man who wants to be successful.

> *If you don't work hard to grow your sales numbers, there could be a situation where the numbers you have already may start depleting.*

The issue with some salespeople is The Comfort Zone Syndrome. They like comfort so much that they don't want any discomfort. A good example of this is when a salesperson develops twenty customers in a given area and does nothing to expand that number. He goes to the field daily on a routine basis to attend to his twenty customers because he believes it's convenient and easier for him. If you don't work hard to grow your sales numbers, there could be a situation where the numbers you have already may start depleting. Competitors' activities might make you lose some of your customers, this is not your prayer, but it does happen.

Just pause a while and think, would you say that all the people who started buying from you when you started are still buying from you today? I am sure not. The truth is that customers encounter a lot of salespeople daily; they listen to many presentations from these salesmen, they also see a lot of competing products. These scenarios affect your selling as a salesman. Some of the customers might decide to switch to your competitors for one reason or the other. Sales job is not a *tea party*, it's a serious business and you need to be alert all the time. This means that you need to work tirelessly to sustain the customers you have already by going the extra mile to delight them. It also means that you need to be working hard daily to increase your customer base. You also need to work diligently to replace lost customers. In sales profession, it is not allowed that you should lose any customer, you must do you best to ensure you keep your customers. But when they are lost because of one reason or the other, then you must work out a strategy to ensure your customer base remain on the increase; the number of your customers shouldn't deplete.

You don't have to wait until you lose a customer before finding a way to get a new client. You should develop a pattern in your mind that assumes that you need to replace a customer that may be lost today or in the future. This does not mean that you will stop being nice to your customers, it means you are just being proactive. Successful people make provision for everything. They plan ahead of time to avoid getting into troubled waters. The best way to be effective in selling is to be at your best in serving your customers and working hard daily to develop new ones. This should be an attitude.

JUST MAKE IT HAPPEN!

Our company once got a job to help position a Quick-Service Restaurant that is new in Lagos. We started the job using our best strategies. Part of what I did to help achieve results faster was to endorse the restaurant. I devised a means to promote them in various platforms associated with me. I talked about the eatery on the social media, on-air, even in our training events. I also ensured that the restaurant served food in meetings organized by our company.

On one occasion, I was part of an event planning committee meeting as the chairman, and the welfare sub-committee needed to order for food for those in attendance. I offered to assist in that regard because the welfare sub-committee chairman wasn't familiar with the neighborhood - to know where and how to get the food, so offering to assist at that time was a noble act. I told the committee that I knew of an eatery that could deliver food to us before the end of the meeting. They were all relieved that the issue had been solved.

I quickly called the manager of the restaurant and informed him about the order. I told them to deliver the food in forty-five minutes. The time I gave them for delivery was possible because the restaurant is situated in Ikeja and our meeting took place in Ikeja. But you can't predict the busy Lagos road!

Lagos is quite a busy place, getting the delivery done within that time was possible, but not that easy; considering the fact that they would need to get the food ready, get on the road and maneuver their way through the busy Lagos traffic. It would require an attitude of exceptional efficiency to meet up with the time. On the other hand, I wanted to use that occasion to try the delivery competence of the quick-service restaurant.

As soon as I had placed the order, I began to monitor them on phone every five minutes to know the position of things. The manager I spoke with earlier - later called me on phone to explain that achieving the forty-five minutes delivery time might not be workable because the food was not ready. As a top salesman, I didn't want to give him the opportunity to *unleash* reasons the food won't be ready. Folks often give a lot of reasons for poor

> *Folks often give a lot of reasons for poor performance and most of the times the reasons are not cogent.*

performance and most of the times the reasons are not cogent. After speaking with the manager, I told myself something had to be done to make the food ready. Our meeting was still on, when the meeting came to a close; that would be the time to serve the food. So I was aware of the situation. I didn't want to give any excuse for not delivering the food in good time.

I called the restaurant manager again and asked him to give the phone to the chef, which he did. By the time I called the manager this time, we had spent about fifteen minutes in our forty-five minutes. When the phone got to the chef, I asked him a simple question: "Is the food ready?" And the chef replied, yes sir, I will serve it in two minutes. Wow! I like good news, that answer made my day. I was not there at the restaurant to monitor things myself; I needed somebody to tell me "It is possible!" I wasn't looking for excuses for not being able to meet my expectations. I had sold the services of the eatery already to the committee, I had told them about their delicious meals and their ability to deliver on time, and I couldn't afford any form of failure. So accepting any excuse that will portray a different picture from the one I had created was not ideal; so the chef was my hero!

About thirty minutes after speaking with the chef, behold the food arrived! They came in at the right time, the meeting agenda had come to a conclusion and the Welfare Committee Chairman approached me for the meal. The service team from the restaurant came in the time the Welfare Committee was asking for the food. The deal was done as planned and expectations were met. I later showed appreciation to the chef the next day by giving him an autographed copy of my book because of the role he played.

The art of selling is a process that leads to closing a deal. It is not easy to get to the closing stage of selling. You must play your part to ensure you close the sale properly. Closing sales require mastery and action. You must know the art. You must know the questions to ask and how to listen for the right answers. You must know the needs of the prospect and find ways to provide the best products or services that will proffer solutions to those needs. This is what you seek to achieve in closing a sale. Closing a sale is beyond writing an invoice; closing a sale is finally arriving at the solutions that will satisfy the prospect. This is why you must take this stage seriously because when it is marred, the sales process fails!

> *Closing a sale is beyond writing an invoice; closing a sale is finally arriving at the solutions that will satisfy the prospect.*

I had all these in mind when I was at the committee meeting. I didn't want to allow any space for failure. I needed to follow the restaurant manager up the way I did. Successful salesmen find ways to fix stuff. They don't find the next excuse for failure. They find solutions. Try not to be an *Excuse Manufacturer!* Promise your prospects and customers the best products and services and find ways to fulfill your promises. Quit excuses. Find solutions!

RIGHT AWAY!

I once listened to one of Brian Tracy's teaching sessions where he talked about "Right Away." He encouraged salesmen to learn the habit of saying right away to their customers or prospects any time they needed to supply products or to perform an assignment. Right Away is applied in several scenarios. When your customer or prospect asks if you can deliver within two hours, don't say, I can't, or let me think about it; say Right Away!

> *There is nothing you cannot achieve, if only you believe and take the right actions. What is within you is beyond the things in your environment that scare you.*

It is better you say right away and come back to your closet and plan how to make it work, than saying it's not possible! I teach Motivational Selling. We teach salespeople to build mindsets that believe they can achieve every tough task. There is nothing you cannot achieve, if only you believe and take the right actions. What is within you is beyond the things in your environment that scare you.

I have discovered over the years that the things that are impossible are the things that are yet to be tried. When you believe it's not possible, it won't be possible; even the ant will make it impossible for you. When you believe it's attainable, no giant can stop you!

You have a lot of abilities within you but you must rise above your fears. A lot of folks fail to achieve their dreams because they are afraid to fail. Fear discourages people from pursuing their dreams. It makes people to stagnate and imagine things without doing the right things.

Successful people go for what they want and get it done. Once you know you are on the right path, then take action and make your dreams come true. This is the mindset I set in motion anytime I want to embark on a big project. This is why we were able to host the first Nigeria Sales

> *You have a lot of abilities within you but you must rise above your fears.*

Conference that was a huge success. The conference that assembled over 2,000 people couldn't have been a success if I didn't believe in the dream and took necessary actions that will make the dream a reality. I often say that success is a deliberate design. You must work your way to the top. You only need to be alert in the mind and take the right actions. When a great idea comes your way, give it the necessary thought and take action right away. The right away formula is the method of champions. It creates an atmosphere of achievement.

The true story about the eatery tells the attitude of two different personalities working in the same organization. The manager didn't know about the Right Away approach, but the chef Knew. Buyers want answers and not the reasons for poor performance. They have needs in the first place that was why they came to you for a solution. You are a solution provider and not an excuse manufacturer! Remember, they have array of choices to make; so giving them excuses is telling them to try elsewhere.

Wait a minute! I am not saying that salesmen should build castles in the sky by saying things that are technically unattainable. When assignments are practically unachievable, it's a different issue. I am not saying that salespeople should accept that they can supply goods from Lagos to Owerri or from New York to Texas within twenty minutes when they know that flights to such distance would take more time than that. A salesman who accepts to do so without thinking of an alternative may be a magician! But most times, this is not the issue. The issue with some salespeople is not leaving their comfort zone; they don't like pushing further. They are comfortable with the way things are, so no need of making any more efforts to change results.

I have learned over the years that we surprise ourselves when we attempt things we have not done before. I have said it before that the difference between greatness and average is just a thin line, and that thin line is called, The Extra Mile. This extra mile is not for everyone, it's meant for the few who want to succeed. If you want to be successful in what you do, you must locate the extra mile. You must find ways to do things differently. You must do a little more than the normal. Folks don't celebrate normal result. People talk about the man or woman who does extraordinary things. You can be celebrated if you can go the extra mile.

> People talk about the man or woman who does extraordinary things. You can be celebrated if you can go the extra mile.

In rendering services or supplying to the customer or prospect, the salesman might experience situations where it won't be feasible to deliver specifications of the buyers. This could be as a result of technical reasons or other causes. If delivering within a particular time frame is technically not possible, the salesman will know and that would take a different approach. The salesperson should seek a way out when he encounters such situations. He should look for a way to seek extension of time of delivery or a way to make the buyer go for alternative product that can be delivered within the time that is convenient for the buyer. It is better you *underpromise* and *overperform* than to *overpromise* and *underperform*.

Say what you can do, don't promise what you know you can't achieve. Eagles can soar high in the sky. Don't expect eagles to swim! You know what is achievable and what is not. But in challenging situations, find ways to make things work even if it means stretching to other alternatives. Don't say to a prospect or customer "It is not possible or we will not meet up with your standard," Instead say, "We don't have that specification now but we have a better alternative" or "It is not technically workable to deliver the kind of quality you are looking for within this time frame but I can give you a good alternative." Remember, salesmen are solution providers and not *excuse manufacturers*.

> *It is better you underpromise and overperform than to overpromise and underperform.*

Right Away is a workable guide for salespeople. Develop the mechanism within - to say Right Away when a customer says, "Can you deliver in twenty-four hours?" Say: Yes! And make it work. Don't say Yes without taking action. Don't say Yes and fail to follow up. Say, Yes and get it done.

BUYERS BUY FROM EXPERTS

John Maxwell says "*Smart people don't know everything, but they know people that do.*" No man is an Island, as the wise saying goes. In business, sometimes you may be required to collaborate with other businesses to execute a task. The main aim is to execute the deal and everyone is happy.

Successful people sometimes depend on assistance from other parties that will help them deliver at various points. But in practice, it may not be ideal to reveal reliance on another person's outcome before delivering your own result. It is not in your best interest to amplify your weakness. It is better you recognize your weakness and play it down. Don't dwell on the things that make you weak. Sing your strengths and

> *It is not in your best interest to amplify your weakness.*

your weakness will dwindle. This is my rule on the negotiation table.

Your closing techniques in your selling should be a total package that portrays you to the buyer as providing the total package, unless it is a situation where your client is aware you are working with other partners or in a situation your clients demands to know your partners. Some information you let out to the buyer might not be necessary; it will only make the salesperson appear unprepared. This does not mean that you are concealing information; it only means application of Sales Wisdom and being tactful. It had been said earlier in this book that it is better to do more listening than talking. Less talk and more listening win the sale. Be a strategic communicator. Talk less, ask and listen more, in order to make your prospect talk more. This is how to sell professionally.

> Talk less, ask and listen more, in order to make your prospect talk more. This is how to sell professionally.

Let me share this true story with you to buttress my point. Jackie [not real name] works for a branding company that we recommended to one of our clients for branding jobs. Her company had passed through all the processes and was awarded the job. The event occurred on a Thursday afternoon when I went for an official meeting with the CEO of the company that awarded the job to Jackie's company. Our company consults for them. We had barely started our meeting when Jackie came in the company of the graphic team of her organization, they had come to discuss some technical issues concerning the job and Jackie who works in the Finance Department joined them to discuss part payment for the job. Jackie was neither a salesperson nor a graphic expert. She was in the right place at the wrong time!

Accordingly, the CEO asked me to join him in the meeting with Jackie's team. During the meeting, the CEO asked a question to ascertain why the fee was high on a particular job. When Jackie heard the question, she was eager to answer but without being equipped with the right answer. She astonishingly replied the CEO saying, "Sir, you know we don't have the capacity to execute all these jobs alone as a company, we are a small company and rely on other organizations for assistance, that's why the fee is high. She continued her expression, "You see Sir, we need to pay other parties, this is how we arrived at the amount we quoted for you." Astonishing! I didn't expect such response from Jackie.

The CEO who was a detailed person, smiled and said jokingly, "But you don't look small." He continued, now pointing at the staff identity card on Jackie's neck, he said, "People who are small don't put on beautiful staff identify cards." We all laughed over it but I saw a big issue in Jackie's answer. I also saw beyond the CEO's hilarious remarks. I saw a big gap in the definition of "The promise to perform" and "Actual ability to perform." I knew that the CEO would be imagining if the company actually has the capability to do the job? The truth is that the company is reliable and creative. We use them for our corporate branding. We wouldn't have recommended them if they were not good. So Jackie's response to the CEO wasn't necessary.

As a trainer, I make use of every advantage to teach people; I didn't wait for the next day to tell Jackie that she could have done better. People want to do business with experts. People want to associate with the best suppliers, the best salespeople, and the best in everything. Most buyers want to buy the best, so it's your duty to prove that you are among the best.

It would have been better for Jackie to have kept quiet for the right person in the team to respond to the CEO. A better answer would have been, "The price is not high sir, this is the best price the job can go for, because of the good quality we are offering, and the process it will pass through to attain your specification." The CEO wouldn't want to go down on his standard. He wouldn't want to go for an inferior quality, so such answer would likely take care of the matter.

You have not misrepresented your company, or misguided the client when you answer from a position of strength. Your duty is to speak the truth without exposing your weakness. You need to make your customer feel he is in safe hands. Remember that the customer entered into the deal believing that you have all it takes to get things done. He didn't get into the business with the hope that you would depend on a third party to deliver his job. It is not the customer's business to get involved in your dealings with a third party - even when you have to rely on that third party before completing the job. The contract is between you and your client, and not between your client and a third party. You must get this clear.

Mentioning a third party the way Jackie did wasn't necessary, it won't add any accolade to their company's profile. Your duty as a salesperson is to get the job done and make the customer happy. You are not under obligation to tell your customer who will help you do the job, but you are under obligation to delight the customer. You need to apply a lot of wisdom in your selling. Wisdom is defined as correct application of knowledge. You need a lot of it to excel in your career.

SING THE FEATURES, SHOW THE ADVANTAGES, AND CELEBRATE THE BENEFITS!

I am an advocate of, Attitude Based and Relationship Selling. I believe that the attitude of the salesman contributes to a very large extent the outcome of the selling. The attitude of the salesman makes or mars the sales process. The salesman who has great self-confidence, and is passionate in his selling will likely be successful. I believe that the more the salesman develops friends in his prospects and customers, the more he sells. I believe also that the integrity of the salesman is the irrefutable quality that leads to sales success. The more straightforward the salesperson is, the more he sells. Buyers like buying from truthful people. I agree totally in this philosophy.

I believe in the saying: "Features tell and Benefits sell." This expression could not be far from the truth. Features, Advantages and Benefits [FAB] of a given product are essential in its selling. Features will tell characteristics of the products, Advantages will tell the importance of the features, they say what the features do. Benefits will make the buyer buy the product. Benefit is the main reason people buy. Benefit is the thing that will close the sale.

This means that if you want to close more sales, you must highlight the benefits in the products and services you are selling. You must show the buyer *What is in it for him*. The buyer should be able to see a great deal in your offering before making his buying decision. The buyer will summarize the features and advantages in a way they will mean benefits to him. The simple logic is that customers buy, they are not sold to. They buy when they see reasons to buy; and they buy for their own reasons and not that of the salesperson. They don't buy because you want them to buy; they buy because they want to buy! It is your duty as a salesman to be on the same page with the buyer. It is your duty to make a convincing presentation that will make him see your offering as the best deal in town.

Let your prospects and customers see why they should buy your product. Give him believable reasons to buy from you. Make the buyer see your products and services from the angle that he stands to lose if he fails to buy from you. What will do the *magic* are the benefits customers see in the product and the way the salesman sells to him.

BE ON THE SAME PAGE WITH THE BUYER

Jeffrey Gitomer says, if you can establish common ground with your prospects, they will like you, trust you, and buy from you. I agree with this thought. It takes an agreement between parties before a sale is made. This agreement should be mutual if there will be a repeat business. If the salesperson takes advantage of the buyer in the first purchase, there may not be another purchase; so the ideal sale is the one in which the agreement is mutual and the parties are happy in the transaction, this is what brings repeat purchase.

The agreement between parties takes a process before the parties will be in one accord. The salesperson should show the buyer what will make him believe in what he is selling. The basic principle of selling is, showing features, illuminating advantages, and selling benefits. This principle is a practical thing; the salesperson should prove it to the buyer. I always ask salespeople who come to sell to me to explain why they want me to buy their products. Some salespeople will say that their product is beautiful. Saying that a product is beautiful without explaining further - won't make someone like me to buy that product. What makes the product beautiful? How reliable is the product? Would the product be attractive today and be unappealing the next day? Salespeople should be able to ask themselves these questions and provide the answers before going to the prospect. Buyers want clear answers to these questions; a salesman who has the answers will definitely smile home. A salesman who is able to connect the buyer with, features, advantages and benefits of his product is likely going to win the sale.

In every buying decision, the buyer is looking out to fill a gap. A good salesperson looks out to connect with the buyer in this area.

In prospecting, qualifying, building rapport and needs identification processes of selling, your mission as a salesperson is to discover the buyer and his intent. When you have discovered what the buyer is thinking, you close in immediately with an inspiring sales presentation. You are like an army commander in the battlefield who discovers the weakness of his opponent. Once the commander discovers the weak spot of his opponent, he moves in immediately with his men. This strategy is also ideal in selling; you don't allow any gap when you have discovered an opening to fill in the buyer's mind. These gaps could be the desires of the buyer, his wants or needs. You discover this by asking the right questions when you are qualifying the prospect. When you have identified these gaps, use the FAB approach as a strategy to sell. Your approach should be to identify these gaps first and fill them by presenting solutions through Features, Advantages and Benefits.

In your sales process, try to find out the FAB that will *fly*. You must sell what the prospect wants. A man who wants to reduce weight may not be in a hurry to buy into the benefits of saving more money if he buys red meat. He will surely prefer other alternatives that will be healthier for him. Capitalize on the needs of the buyer and what will attract him to buy. The thing that will attract him to buy will in turn be the benefit of buying the product. This has a direct connection.

I always advocate that salespeople should know their products beyond features. Most salesmen will tell the buyer what the product is made of, but will fail to take that explanation to the next level of explaining the advantages of those features and the benefits it will bring to the buyer if he buys the product.

Let us look at this story. I once, went with Maureen to replace our generating set for power supply. We got to a shop that sells generating sets and saw two kinds of the product. We didn't have any particular type in mind. The two generating sets looked alike. The products share same features; both can be operated manually or with a key, both are also sound proof. The prices of the products were almost similar, though product A [the first one we saw] was slightly more expensive. We didn't notice any significant disparity in the two products to aid us in making a decision; the difference was technical which would require an expert to understand.

The owner of the shop later took time to explain the difference in the products. He explained that the features of the two products are almost similar but the main distinction in the two was the coil. Product A was made of copper coil, while Product B was made of aluminum coil. He told us that the one made of copper was more durable because, the aluminum coil could easily get rusty while the copper won't. He explained that coil is a vital component in a generating set; once the coil is good, the product will likely last longer.

His explanations made sense to us. The shop owner's explanation summarized that product A would be more durable than product B. It also meant that we will not buy another generating set for a long time, thereby saving money [benefit] in the course of time. We did not wait for further explanations, we got the benefit we were looking for and we closed the deal.

WHEN YOU DISCOVER; YOU RECOVER

One of the definitions of Philosophy I cherish is, "Quest for knowledge." This definition portrays the subject Philosophy as an unending search for knowledge. Jeffrey Gitomer, said, *"There are billions of 'customer types.' Want to sell them all? You can do it in five words: Look. Question. Listen. Harmonize. Practice."* I will use the word "Discover," to summarize these five words. It is when you look, question and listen to a prospect that you will discover. It is what you have discovered that you will work to harmonize, go with and begin to practice. It takes discovery before recovery. You cannot take charge of what you have not discovered. You can only discover what you have explored.

> *It takes discovery before recovery. You cannot take charge of what you have not discovered.*

Salespeople make the mistake of being in a hurry to sell their products first before discovering the prospect. Slow down. You just need to take it easy here. It is true that you are under pressure to meet up with your sales target, it is true that you need to close the sale; but it is also imperative that you allow the buyer sell to you first before selling to him! The buyer sells to you when you slow down during your sales conversation to understand what he really wants.

It has been expressed that the sales process is an agreement between parties. There has to be a mutual agreement before the sale. When the parties involved fail to agree, sales may not take place, even when it does, there might not be repeat sales. The main duty of the salesman is to agree with the buyer. When the salesman and the buyer genuinely agree to transact, then the relationship begins. This is the ideal way to begin; strike a genuine agreement with the buyer. Don't take advantage of the buyer. Selling is a mutual deal.

Try also to think through the perspective of the prospect or customer. Appreciate his situation even when you know you are at his place for business. A prospect that has just lost money in a new business venture will naturally be unhappy. You need to understand emotional intelligence to deal with this type of prospect. People are happy and relaxed when you show care and love to them. People management and emotional intelligence are great skills in selling.

Bringing up sales conversation at the wrong time will be counterproductive, self-centered and insensitive. Make your presentations at the right time but not when the prospect or customer is emotionally indisposed to listen to you.

When you connect with people emotionally, you discover them. You discover the real person when you tap into his emotion. If you know his emotional make-up, you will be better disposed to know how to transact with the person. The popular sales maxim says that people buy emotionally and justify logically. A prospect might decide to buy from you just because you connected with him emotionally. Connecting with prospects emotionally can only be done by a salesman who is not in a hurry to sell. If you are in a hurry to sell, you might not notice when the prospect is not in the best frame of mind. You know what? Most salesmen who hurriedly want to sell to prospects are likely going to hurry out without a sale!

The Selling Champion connects with his target audience. He connects with the prospects first and shows him the benefits in his products before trying to sell. In personal selling, you should first discover who the prospect is, what he is, and his personality type and so on. Always remember that selling is an art and science. The investigatory aspect of selling requires that you discover the prospect. Discover why he buys and why he does not. This aspect of selling is not achieved by talking too much; it is achieved by smartly observing the prospect to know his or her disposition.

> People buy you when you buy them first. They understand you when you have understood them.

Successful salespeople connect. Try to find out what is happening in the prospect's life. You sell faster and easier when you have bought your prospect's piece of mind. People *buy* you when you *buy* them first. They understand you when you have understood them. What matters in selling is the prospect's perspective and not necessarily that of the salesman. The salesman's strategy might be the best in the world but the prospect might not be in the mood to buy. A salesman who finds himself in this situation should connect with the prospect first before trying to sell. Try to creatively find out why he is not in the best mood to buy. If you can unravel what is in his mind, then you get closer to beginning a successful sales expedition.

A mother who wants to feed a crying baby will first find out why the baby is weeping and probably stop the crying before feeding the baby. Selling takes this approach too. You don't sell to a prospect you have not connected with; whether emotionally or otherwise. Create a buying situation first. Don't push too hard to sell when you know the prospect is preoccupied with other issues. Discover him first. The more you discover what is happening inside the prospect's world and are in agreement with him, the easier it is for you to know the prospect. The closer you get to the prospect, the better you discover him. The more you discover the prospect, the more you find out his needs and the solution for them. The more you provide solutions for his needs, the more the prospect buys and continues to buy. It is that simple!

BEFORE YOU TALK, HAVE THE FLOOR

During my early years in the art of speaking, I was an upcoming speaker, although I had spoken on big stages but I would prefer to say I was still announcing my presence at the time. I remember the experience I had when I was invited to speak to the National Youth Corps Members at their Orientation Camp in Lagos. The Head of Library Department of the National Youth Service Corps [NYSC] had approached me to mentor some corps members with the aim of improving their reading culture. I have a Pet project: Read a Page [RAP] which seeks to encourage individuals to open an educative book and read a page daily. My aim with RAP is to raise two hundred thousand readers annually. We use various platforms to promote the project. So my team went to the NYSC Orientation Camp to promote the concept.

We got there and met about three thousand corps members. Yes, three thousand people; for a speaker who was still climbing the ladder! The organizers had told me that my speaking time was ten minutes. I felt the time was too short. I tried to extend the time but the officials maintained they had other speakers who would be speaking on various topics and the time allowed was ten minutes for each speaker. The allotted time was an issue; it won't be an easy task to send my message across within ten minutes. However, I have trained myself as a salesman to face any task without being dispirited - once I have decided to embark on such mission; so I decided to move on with the assignment.

My first rule in selling which is also same in speaking is to take over the environment within the first thirty seconds. In order to succeed in this type of environment, I must invent a strategy that will catch attention faster within that short period. I told my team we would have failed in the assignment once we lose the crowd within the first few seconds. So I decided to start my opening by giving. Giving is good always; it opens doors, I decided to give out three autographed copies of my books to the first three people who will answer my question correctly. My question was simple. I asked the audience to mention the author and title of a book they had read that month. We subsequently concluded the segment within the first 3 minutes. I got answers and signed autographs for the 3 corps members who answered the question. The beginning was creative enough because the audience applauded the corps members who received the books. The remaining minutes was *fun*! We succeeded because we had the floor. The Assistant Director of NYSC who listened to my presentation later commended my approach; she said my style engaged the corps members.

My aim at the event was to take charge of the environment before I start and that was achieved because of the style we adopted.

In the story, the youth corps members were my prospects. It was either I get their attention and sell to them or I don't, and fail. Jeffrey Gitomer puts it this way; *"Don't start any kind of sales conversation until you are certain that they are ready and willing. Ready to listen and willing to receive the message."* This thought can't be more correct.

One of our staff complained to me some years ago that the prospect I introduced to him refused to buy. I didn't want to tell the salesman that he was not getting something right; instead I offered to visit the prospective buyer with him to find out why he had not bought. When we got there, Ikechukwu Okolie smiled when he sighted me from a distance and said, "Your salesman is always coming when I am busy and he is always in a hurry to leave." I immediately knew the reason he had not bought. The salesman wanted the prospect to buy at his own time and not the prospect's time!

The first rule in any society is orderliness. This is also same in business. This is why there are structures in standard organizations, which tells who does what. In selling, the salesman should first achieve this orderliness before beginning the sales conversation. People buy when they are ready to buy. They listen when they don't have any other thing distracting them from listening. They are interested when they have listened to you and understood what you are saying. They buy when what you say makes sense to them. This sequence will only take place in an environment where the buyer and the seller have agreed to listen to each other.

A salesman who walks into a business premises to make a supply and sees the owner of the business arguing with another party - should be courteous enough to put on hold supplying the products at that moment, unless the owner of the business gives him a go ahead to supply. The salesman may not get involved in settling the dispute but the salesman is supposed to sit and wait to be attended to. Never hurry out and feel that the prospect or customer is taking your time, be patient. Be relaxed and happy. Don't express any form of urgency.

A salesman selling to an unhappy buyer stands a risk of not closing the deal if he fails to manage the situation properly. The threat the salesman may experience in this kind of situation is the risk of losing the sale and by extension, losing the customer. The buyer who is already in a bad mood might decide to transfer his anger to the salesman if the salesman is not outstanding in his style of selling. Remember the rule: the customer is always right, you can't win an argument with a customer; even if you do, you lose the customer!

The next time you visit a prospect, make sure he is in the mood to listen. I don't like wasted sales outings. No salesman is expected to be happy when he prepares for a sales conversation only to fail. Find out why the sales meeting did not hold. Did you come at the right time or were you trying to hold the meeting at your own time and not the buyer's?

The ship does not move except the coast is clear. The airplane won't take off in a turbulent weather. Don't start any sales conversation if you don't have the "ears" and the "eyes" of the buyer. Ensure that you get his attention before you start your presentation. People buy your story when you catch their attention, not when they are distracted. Apply this fundamental rule and be a successful salesman.

> *The ship does not move except the coast is clear. The airplane won't take off in a turbulent weather. Don't start any sales conversation if you don't have the "ears" and the "eyes" of the buyer.*

ASK RIGHT, SELL RIGHT

In sales conversation, the salesman is selling "YES" to the buyer or prospect, and the buyer or prospect is selling "No" to the salesman. If the salesman's strategy of selling YES is not strong enough, he may have to buy the No from the prospect!

> *If the salesman's strategy of selling YES is not strong enough, he may have to buy the No from the prospect!*

The art of buying and selling is like a game arena. The parties have their strategies and everyone wants to prove a point. The salesman wants to show the buyer that his product is the best and the buyer wants to buy the best product at the best bargain.

Sometimes, it might not be easy for the salesman to know what the buyer wants. The salesman might be wondering and wishing for a lot of things, may be yearning to know the best way to present his product to the buyer or the best approach to use in a given situation. You can't sell by guessing, you must strike on target. You need to know what's going on in the buyer's mind and one of the best techniques to apply in this aspect is asking the right questions. This has been explained earlier. Get the answers from the prospects by asking them the right questions. The more questions the salesman asks the easier and closer he gets to the closing.

Prospects are in their own world, they are approached daily by many salesmen with a lot of products and services. These salespeople come with different sales strategies, so the buyer is faced with the challenge of making the best decision. This is the issue most of the time. The questions now are: How do you help the prospect make the best decision? How do you make him tell you what he is not saying? How do you unravel the unspoken words? The answer is simple, ask the right questions and listen attentively!

Once you are able to discover what is going on in the prospect's mind, then you are almost close to the sale.

> *Once you are able to discover what is going on in the prospect's mind, then you are almost close to the sale.*

Buyers don't say everything most of the times, they want to see what you are bringing to the table first; the offer you are coming with. They want to compare your offer with that of the salesman who just left their premises! Prospects want to know the difference in the two offerings. Most times, the difference in two products is the salesman; the salesman makes the difference. The products or services might be similar but the man behind the sales makes the difference. The salesman's approach defines the difference.

The salesperson makes the difference by his personality and style of selling. You need to create a unique character and method of selling. The type that will open every door, the style that makes prospects believe you came to add value to their businesses. Your method of selling should portray you as a friend, and not just a salesman. The buyer should see you as a helper who has come to assist him to grow.

In trying to find out what the buyer is not saying in order to close the sale, approach it from an angle of a helper.

Suppose you met a prospect who commenced a new business and you have a policy in your company that allows thirty days credit sales for new businesses. Let's look at the following illustration of a prospective customer Charity, who runs a superstore, and a salesman, who sells cosmetics. The salesman is meeting the prospect for the first time.

Salesman: "Hello Charity, you have a big place here, I can see that the place is new."

Charity: "Not really, but we are fairly new; we are 8 months old here."

Salesman: "Oh! That's great. You have a good location, I believe business is flourishing."

Charity: "Oh yes, we are doing pretty well."

NB: Here the salesman takes note of 8 Months and Pretty Well. Doing well in business within 8 months of commencement means that the salesman is talking to the right prospect.

Salesman: Looking round the premises and observing carefully, the salesman says, "Your cosmetics product range is not much from what I see on your shelves, it seems your stock has gone down on cosmetics."

NB: Here, the salesman acts as a friend who cares that the prospect's range of cosmetics is not enough. This will make the prospect develop in her mind a feeling of acceptance that the salesman wants to assist her business to grow. The question is likely going to create a relaxed mood for the prospect which will make her see the salesman as someone who is on her side. This is a plus for the salesman. The duty of the salesman is to create a win-win situation - where the prospect thinks he is safe in his hands.

Charity: "Eemm, our supplier is supplying two varieties for now, but ... what line of products do you have?"

Note: The salesman should be alert to expressions; both spoken and unspoken. Observe body language, eye movement, tapping fingers on the table, etc. When these are taking place, the prospect is communicating something that he or she is not speaking out. He is consulting with the *innerchamber* of his mind where all the decisions are taken. This is an opportunity to close the sale. The salesman who is alert will close in immediately at this vital stage and ask for the order. Once the prospect gets interested at this stage, the sale is closed. When the prospect made the expression, "eemm," it could mean that she wasn't totally satisfied with the offer she got from her current suppliers. When she asked the salesman "What line of products do you have?" The salesman should know that a buying signal has come.

Salesman: "We have many varieties of products..., we are also willing to give you all the product ranges you want; we believe you need these varieties to build your business at this stage. We are willing to work with you in this area."

Note: Here the salesman acts as a solution provider. Saying they are *willing* to give and *willing* to work with Charity, are open offers to assist the prospect. The prospective customer will open her ears, eyes and mind to hear more. This is another good point for the salesman. Again, the salesman has taken an upper hand in the sales conversation. He has put himself in a position where the prospect will be struggling to buy! Salesmen should always create this kind of atmosphere.

Charity: "We need all the products you mentioned, but we need to know your payment method."

Note: The prospect will likely need the products because every buyer wants more good products in order to make more profit. The salesman's offer is also attractive because the current supplier is not providing enough products to the superstore; apparently the buyer's payment pattern does not suit the current suppliers. Note also that the prospect brought up the issue of payment mode. She was trying to qualify the salesman on their payment policy when she said, "But we need to know your payment method." Again, this is another good point for the salesman, this is now the opportunity to offer the thirty days credit sales lifeline.

Salesman: "Okay, looking at the situation, we will offer you the entire product you need and allow thirty days for payment. We believe we can grow together. What do you think?" The salesman may also decide not to allow the entire thirty days credit sales lifeline at a go. He may offer seven days, fourteen days or twenty-one days. This is good in negotiation. It will help the salesman to negotiate better. It will also work to the salesman's advantage in a case of default in paying within the agreed time.

Note: Always keep the sales rule that says, "Never get caught Selling!" Don't be caught selling. The salesman should present himself in a way the prospect would want to buy, not in a situation where he will be under pressure to sell. Don't make it too obvious that you have come to sell.

In the scenario, Charity would believe the salesman is doing her a favour. The salesman presented his proposal in a way that shows his company would want to start a great business relationship that will be of benefits to both parties; this is what every prospect wants to hear. People like win-win deal. Note also that the salesman did not lose his comportment when he saw that the prospective customer wanted his products. He still ended his offer with a question, "What do you think?" This question depicts the salesman's confidence; it also seeks to get a confirmation from the prospect that she is happy with the offer and ready for a robust business relationship. I call this, "Super Close Question." You use this technique when you have taken charge of the sales conversation. You use the technique to make the prospect to ask for the product. Let the prospect request for the supply; don't dump it on him or her! Prospects value products and services they asked for, than when the products were *forced* on them. Experience taught me this. You also need to be careful where you use the technique. You may not necessarily use the method when you are still establishing yourself in the process. Use *super close question* when you have gained grounds and when you have got the *undivided attention* of the prospect or customer. The approach helps the salesman to qualify the prospect further on the ability to pay for his product. It also puts the prospect in a position where he or she will be the one asking for the product and not where the salesman is struggling to sell.

Charity: "Do you have the products in your vehicle? Can you supply now?"

Salesman: "Right away!"

You will notice that this sequence began with observing properly and asking the right questions. The salesman in the illustration did not come in like a salesman; he came in like a friend and a helper. You attract people when they are convinced that they are safe in following you. Salesmen should stop selling and start creating buying situations! When you depend so much only on your sales pitch, you have not made any difference; other salesmen do that too. When you position yourself where you will attract the prospect or customer to buy; you define the difference. This is the distinction between top salespeople and average salespeople. Take a position now.

LET THE BUYER OWN IT BEFORE HE BUYS

Great thinkers are in agreement that: "We are what we think." Human nature sometimes or even most times imagines things they wish to happen. Folks dream of things they wish to have which creates a desire to own such things in their minds. This imagination triggers actions that control the human nature.

> *What you desire to have becomes your fantasy.*

What you desire to have becomes your fantasy. Let me share this story with you. I have a friend who is a successful entrepreneur; let's identify him in this story with his title - Chief. Chief is in love with the latest model of Ford Explorer and asked me on one occasion to accompany him to a car shop to enquire about the vehicle. We got to the car shop and Chief saw the vehicle he was looking for. The interior was great and roomy; the vehicle was quite exclusive and beautiful - the features met his specifications. I believe Chief must have been dreaming about that vehicle for a long time before that day - because the expression of approval on his face was conspicuous; the sales manager at the car shop saw the expression too. Apparently, Chief was happy that he saw what he was looking for. I smiled because I knew the sales manager has seen a *gap* in a prospect and would want to close it immediately. Chief didn't hide his feeling about the vehicle and a good salesman would take advantage of that. I decided to observe the process. Then the conversation with the sales manager began:

Chief: "How are you today? I think I like the vehicle, I am actually looking for a family size vehicle with this kind of interior. I believe this can take my family to the village this holiday."

Note: Chief created an impression immediately that he likes the vehicle; the expression was psychological. It takes a professional to conceal such expression. Again, Chief didn't hide his feelings on the features, advantage and benefits the vehicle offered - when he talked about liking the size and interior and going to the village with his family in the vehicle. Chief's conspicuous interest had done half of the job for the salesperson!

Sales Manager: Welcome to our place Sir. I know you would like the vehicle! Your family will look great inside this machine this holiday, but we have only one left. Our stock went down three days ago and I am not sure of the exact date we will receive a new shipment of the vehicle. I believe you are ready to buy now. Turning to me, she gave me a warm friendly smile perhaps, to make sure I was not going to oppose her in the sales conversation. I had no intention of bothering her anyway; I had taken that decision earlier. In fairness to her company, the vehicle was actually a machine; great Interior. The vehicle simply stands out! Although I wouldn't have expressed obvious satisfaction if I was to be the prospective customer, I would prefer to keep calm without revealing my eagerness to buy the vehicle.

Note: The Sales Manager created an imagination in the prospect's mind by saying that Chief's family would look great in the vehicle during the holidays. She also communicated the scarcity of the product as a persuasive tool. The vehicle remaining only one would simply arouse Chief's buying interest. It is ideal to communicate near scarcity of a product whenever the product is going out of stock, this will help to guide your customers or prospects in the decision making. In this scenario, the prospective buyer is positive; therefore communicating the actual position of stock is professional. The buyer has shown willingness to own the product looking at what has transpired in the conversation so far. The Sales Manager also qualified the prospect by saying, "I believe you are ready to buy now." She wanted to be sure she was talking to the right person; the ideal prospect. Again, she gave me a warm smile just to get my attention emotionally, at least if I can't speak in her favour, I shut up! Another great score for the Sales Manager. The salesperson made a smart move when she gave me that warm smile. Her gesture depicts: "If you can't support me, please don't work against me." I got that!

Note also: Always ask a creative question or make a creative statement that will lead you closer to the closure. Using the example: When the Sales Manager said "I believe you are ready to buy now" This statement will arouse Chief's consciousness about his interest to own the vehicle, especially when the salesperson had communicated that the vehicle was remaining only one. The prospect's response to this kind of statement will often lead the salesman closer to unraveling other information from the buyer, which will aid in the closing. Your questions or comments should be strategic and on target. Your questions should not be empty, but should create an impression in the prospect's mind. Questions or comments from the salesman should be constructed in a way that it leads to several ways to close the sale. Chief is likely not going to give a negative answer to the salesperson's question because he had bought the vehicle even before the salesperson said hello to him!

Chief: Only one left, and you are not sure when the next consignment is coming? Okay, let me see the manual. What is the payment method? I have seen the price, what's my discount? Can I pay through my bank?

Sales Manager: Sure! We can arrange for payment, how soon can you do that?

Note: Again, the Sales Manager qualifies the ability to pay by asking a question, "How soon can you do that?" The prospect will give an answer that will indicate how soon he wants to pay, whether he is paying through his bank or through any other source. Note also that Chief's interest to have the vehicle was high; he had shown a lot of buying signals by asking many questions at the same time, which exposes desire to own the vehicle. He had bought the vehicle in his mind already! The payment for the vehicle was done the following day. The Sales Manager did an outstanding job.

Your duty is to be an outstanding salesperson. Try to apply smart selling strategies that will lead you to success.

ALWAYS GIVE VALUE

We have a character in our company which is hinged on Excellence. We believe in high quality and Value Creation. We talk about quality before talking about sales. We sell excellence. When we sell products or services, we promote value. If the product or service isn't good; we won't sell! These are the things we consider first before doing any job. This is our attitude. This is our core value. We want to always live up to our company's promise which is: "We Don't Only Satisfy Our Clients; We Delight Them!" What will delight the client is the good quality of your product and the value he derives from it.

I have the permission of Sir Ike Onyechi, CEO Alpha Pharmacy Limited to share this story. He is one of our clients who operates a successful multiple branch network of pharmacies in Nigeria. Alpha Pharmacy is known for the supply of rare ethical drugs for cardiac operations. We once went there to sell our Annual Masterclass to his organization. We had shortlisted the organization as one of the companies we will partner for the business year, so we wanted to sign on with them for mutual benefit. I have a good personal and business relationship with the CEO, which is a great advantage for our company.

On that fateful day, I called Sir Onyechi on phone and we scheduled to meet by 3.00pm in his office. I got to his office around 2.40pm and his Personal Assistant received me but told me to wait a while as her boss was in a meeting with someone. I had prepared my mind for that already because I came a bit early before the scheduled time. I came to his office from another business meeting on Victoria Island, so going straight to his office by that time made business sense because I would still have had to pass through his office before getting to mine.

I usually go out with a book which I read anytime I find myself waiting. So I had a book in my hand: *Speak To Win*, by Brian Tracy, which Brian had autographed for me. I knew I may have to wait for some minutes before seeing the CEO and I didn't want to just wait without doing something; so the book was handy.

Sir Onyechi came out with his guest after about 18 minutes and met me where I was seated and said to me, "George, I know you are waiting, I was in a meeting when you came in." With those few lines, he ushered me into his office. Then the conversation began. We exchanged greetings and talked a little about business and he reminded me how he saw me in Church the previous Sunday.

I had armed myself with a detailed proposal for the deal. I

needed to present a package that would make a lot of business sense. I also needed to enumerate benefits of our proposal. Busy CEOs don't have time to listen to features and advantages; they talk about Benefits! I know you studied Mathematics in the school; the formula needed here is to add up the Features and Advantages to equal Benefit. That is, find a way to collate all the features and advantages to mean benefits that can be touched, seen and experienced. Let the prospect imagine the Benefits in his mind as you speak. I know you won't fail in this arithmetic!

My presentation was simple. I spoke on the four benefits packed into each session of the training that would add value to their brand. The CEO is a renowned Pharmacist and an astute Professional. He watched and listened to me as I concluded my presentation and said, "George a lot of people bring training proposals, most of those proposals fail to give us reasons we should agree with them, but I have seen a lot of value in your presentation. He did something that inspired me to share this story. He picked up the phone and called the General Manager, Sales and Marketing Department and said, "I suppose you know George, The Selling Champion, he is here with a proposal. I have read through the proposal and I am convinced that it has a lot of value in it, I don't mean to take away your job, I know the approval process ought to have started from you but I am sending George to you to look at the proposal, I believe you will agree with me that they are giving us value." He turned to me and said, "George, see the GM and discuss the deal, I believe you won't have any issues when you get there." I thanked him and left for the GMs office. The GM received me as expected and read through the proposal. The expression I heard was, "Wow! This is good! This exclamation coming from the General Manager was an indication of a great offer! And I said to myself, *You can say that again!* We later closed the deal and the business relationship continued thereafter successfully.

If you were the Salesman who experienced this type of sales conversation, what would be your reaction? I believe you will regard that day as one of your best. What sold the proposal were two things:

[1] Good relationship; personal and business. People buy people.

[2] The benefits in the proposal, which the company saw as great value.

People buy value for their money and not beautiful proposals. Proposals should be overloaded with benefits the prospect will derive from the deal. Well-constructed grammar in your proposal that fails to show what is in it for the prospect will end up in the *waste bin*!

> **People buy value for their money and not beautiful proposals.**

Again, whenever you have the opportunity to explore already existing friendly relationships, don't hesitate take the advantage.

People will always prefer to buy from friends they like and trust. This is a general rule in sales. But don't depend only on the friendship that exists between you and the buyer. Ensure you sell value. Ensure that excellence is a way of life for you. Nothing beats performance on the negotiation table. Nothing beats excellence. In the final analysis, people will prefer the best products and services. Ensure you offer outstanding products and services that will standout everywhere.

Give me six hours to chop down a tree, and I will spend the first four sharpening the axe. -Thomas Jefferson

SALES TIPS

1. The result you will achieve in a task is a function of the level of work you have done.
2. It is good to close a sale but it is better to open a relationship first.
3. Before you give up on a task, try one more time.
4. In selling, people don't listen to rhetoric. They listen to results. Show results!
5. Say "Yes" to a prospect, and make your "Yes" work. Happen to things!
6. Buyers buy from experts. Make yourself one.
7. What sells is Benefits. Show it to the prospect.
8. Talk only when you have the prospect's undivided attention.
9. Asking right is selling right.
10. Selling Value is imperative to sales success. Be a person of excellence.

One testimonial is worth one hundred sales pitches.
— Jeffrey Gitomer

CHAPTER SIX
NEVER A ONE-OFF SALE

In business you get what you want by giving other people what they want.
- Alice Macdougall

The first duty of a business is to create customers. This was Peter Drucker's advice to businesspeople over forty years ago. Brian Tracy added that you don't only create customers; you must also seek ways to sustain them. The growth of a business is hinged on the ability of that business to sustain its existing customers and also open up other ways of attracting and retaining new ones.

I have taken time to observe that many indigenous businesses that existed in the 70s and 80s have fizzled out. I believe that part of the reasons for this colossal failure was inability of such businesses to apply the philosophy of attracting, sustaining and expanding customers. Attracting, sustaining and expanding customers in any business should be an attitude. It should be one of the philosophies of any business that wants to outlive its founders. Achieving this status is not rocket science; it's doable.

I have always maintained that it takes two major components for a sale to take place. It takes these two important elements to win a prospect. The first is the attitude of the salesman, and the second, the good quality of the product or service. I have always told salespeople that sales is incomplete if it fails to attract repeat and referral selling. You can't talk about repeat patronage or referral selling without talking about these two elements.

What will determine the referral is your offering in the previous purchase. If the buyer got a great deal the first time, he would become a promoter of your product, he will not only buy again; he will tell his friends and business partners to buy as well. It takes a lot of efforts from the salesman to get to this stage of selling. The salesman would have displayed excellence in his relationship with the customer. You must go the extra mile to win prospects and customers to your side.

Thomas Watson, former IBM CEO says, "*If you don't genuinely like your Customers, chances are they won't buy.*" Customers are the oxygen of the business. You need to make them feel that they are liked and cared for. When they feel this way, then it's a great deal for them. You are assured that the chances of buying elsewhere are very slim. If the deal wasn't good enough then it becomes a one-off sale!

A one-off sale is not the dream of any business. When a salesperson sells once to buyers and fails to sell again, then the business the salesman is representing is in *trouble*! What sustains a business is repeat patronage. The duty of the salesperson is to find out how to achieve this result. Selling as an art posits that the salesperson should make things happen. He should move on until the result is achieved. He should develop friends and influence base in his sales activities. The

> *A one-off sale is not the dream of any business.*

> The more you develop friendship and trust in your relationship with your prospects, the easier it becomes to sell to them.

more you develop friendship and trust in your relationship with your prospects, the easier it becomes to sell to them. The more the salesman is able to command reasonable level of genuine influence on the prospect or customer, the faster they make up their minds to buy from him. This is simple logic, people buy from friends and people they like and trust.

In any buying and selling arena, all the parties involved are selling something to each other. The salesperson is selling his products or services to the prospective buyer. He does this by the way he presents his product. He tries his best to convince the buyer that his product represents the best deal. Same way, the prospective buyer is also selling something to the salesman. The buyer sells his interest, opinion, comfort and needs - to the salesman. He wants to be sure that the salesman's offering is ideal for him.

It is the duty of the salesman to prove his point by showing the prospect the reasons to buy. Sell like a champion! Let the first sale you make lead to the second, the third and so on. Let it lead to consistent repeat purchases and referrals. This is what grows a business. Businesses grow when continuity is assured. One of the ways of ensuring sustainability of a business is consistent patronage from customers. Salesmen should ensure this patronage all the time.

THE ROUTE THAT IS GOOD; CALLS FOR A SECOND JOURNEY

The popular Igbo adage: *An expedition that is good, calls for a second one* - brings to mind that what guarantees a second attempt on a subject is the previous experience on that topic. In a traditional Igbo setting, it is believed that a beautiful and well nurtured bride will always attract admirable suitors, hence the popular Igbo adage: *A good product sells itself.* This wise old saying couldn't be more correct.

A good product for me is a total package. A good product should be seen in the attitude of the salesman who sells the product and the commendable quality of what he is selling. When these two elements are present in one package, it becomes ideal for a repeat purchase; it becomes suitable for continuous patronage.

Whenever you find yourself selling; whether you are selling tangible products or services, never sell for a single invoice. Find a way to open up the next sale during the first sales experience. Always think the next sale in every sale you close. In order to achieve this, the salesman should, be competent, active, creative, interesting, truthful, confident and always adding value. Buyers will prefer to buy from salespeople with these attributes. Do you want to sell to one prospect 50 times at a stretch from the first day you sold to him? Go get these attributes!

> **Always think the next sale in every sale you close.**

Developing an eye for tomorrow's sales takes a visionary salesman. It takes a salesman who believes in himself, his product and his company. It also takes a salesperson who wants to develop a relationship with a prospect to begin the activities of "beautifying a route." A salesman beautifies a route with a prospect by doing everything he can to ensure that the buyer is happy. A happy customer is a repeat

> A happy customer is a repeat customer and the strength of the company.

customer and the strength of the company. When the salesman makes the buyer happy all the time, the buying and selling experience will likely continue.

Making the buyer happy is not an expedition to the moon; it is not rocket science. Making a buyer happy can be achieved through various ways a salesman has developed to satisfy his customers. It could be in the outstanding products and services. It could be in the prompt delivery style of the salesman. It could be in the salesman's personality, it could be in his exceptional positive attitude which attracts people to him; it could also be the trustworthiness of the salesperson. Buyers like buying from truthful people. There are ways to make a buyer happy. The way prospects' faces vary is the way their opinions, preferences, and needs differ. This means that the salesperson needs to apply diverse strategies to achieve buyers' happiness. The salesman needs to approach every individual buyer from a perspective that will ensure a happy customer, and the approach to use for an individual buyer may vary from the other.

I have always maintained that salespeople should avoid generic proposals. Prospects needs differ; therefore solutions to these needs will vary also. It is wise to prepare offerings that will meet these individual needs. This is how to standout as a salesman. You must be unique and resourceful in your selling; giving value and achieving excellent results. This is why I maintain that the ideal salesman is like a movie actor. He fits into every mood and perspective. He smiles, plays, gets emotional, talks and keeps silent when necessary. He gets into various moods to ensure that he satisfies the stakeholders.

Making the prospects or customers happy is a function of the disposition of the salesman. A salesman who likes himself, his product and his job is likely going to be passionate in talking about his product. This is a vital aspect of selling. A happy salesman will always show it in his attitude, in his appearance, in the way he speaks, and in the way he does his job. An unhappy salesperson with low self esteem, oftentimes fail to the temptation of speaking ill of his job. Unhappiness should not be allowed in the world of selling. An unhappy salesman will likely not make a sales champion. Selling requires the best mood because the art of selling is more psychological than technical; it is 80% psychological and 20% technical, as propounded by Brian Tracy. A lot of emotions and feelings take place in selling and they are what determine the sale. You need to connect emotionally with yourself, before transferring that feeling to the prospect. It is when you are happy that you will make the next person happy. You cannot give what you don't have. In all situations, always ensure that you like yourself, your product, your job and your customer. In fact, I like expressing it this way: like yourself, like your Job, like your product and the customer will like you!

Selling is an emotional art; people follow their feeling before they buy. The salesman who succeeds in creating a beautiful atmosphere with the prospect by the way he carries himself, talks about his product and his job or the way he connects with the prospect will likely be successful.

You cannot sell what you don't like. Buyers observe the way you connect with your product. They also observe how passionate you are with your job. They get interested in you and your product when you communicate a lot of passion; when you talk about your product and your job as if they are the best in the world. The salesman who communicates a positive attitude always will likely make happy customers. Create more happy buyers today and keep smiling to the bank! People will often want to repeat a route that is memorable, make yourself the salesman who attracts a repeat purchase.

THE PERSONAL TOUCH

One of the core functions of a Manager is organizing. Some school of thoughts in Management argue that organizing should come before planning while others believe that planning comes before organizing. Some also argue that planning and organization go simultaneously. Whichever way you approach it, you might be right. Ensuring procedures and policies should be part of the planning and organizing stage of the business. In line with this topic, I suggest that salespeople should have a form of organizing and planning before they venture into selling. Selling is no longer an all comers' affair. It is a serious business!

Selling is an art and science, just as mentioned earlier in this book. It takes researching the prospects, the market, the competitors, the products and even yourself, to be able to come out as a "Good-to-go salesman." You need to be as charismatic as possible, be knowledgeable in the job; be detailed in product knowledge and also discover ways to connect with prospects and customers. You can't be wrong in selling when you get these aspects right.

I go to places I will experience personal touch. People like the best products and services. Buyers go out of their way to buy the things that make them happy. I once commended the Vice President of Hub Mart Shopping Mall at GRA Ikeja -

for their unique style of service. I noticed that their client service is exceptional. Their workers attend to customers' needs efficiently. They are very professional. This style is also what I observed when I visited their Adeola Odeku Branch on Victoria Island, Lagos. My experience at Hub Mart made me conclude that the organization spent time to develop a customer friendly brand. Maureen and I patronize the shopping mall because of these outstanding reasons. As a sales and marketing expert, I know a brand that has done a lot of work to distinguish themselves in the marketplace.

Giving personal touch costs nothing. It only takes a little commitment to achieve. It takes the little time you spend to understand how to discover the needs of the customer. It takes your willingness to delight the customer by offering exceptional products and services. It takes the extra mile you go - to fulfill your promises. Ensuring Personal Touch is the way to go in today's tough marketplace. Folks want astounding products and services. Show them you are the best person to provide what they are looking for. Be exceptional. Show Personal Touch in what you do. Go the extra mile to prove you are the best. People will continue to buy from you when you create the right ambiance that ensures repeat purchase. Buying and selling is a mutual deal. Every party in the deal must be happy.

SELL TO ATTRACT ANOTHER

The joy of a traveler is complete when he gets to his destination. Travelling is not complete until the person travelling gets to his destination safely. This also applies in the everyday life of a salesperson. The joy of a successful salesperson is to attract continuous sales. He wishes that the selling experience never ends. He wants to sell and sell and sell!

The Igbos of Nigeria are known for their expertise in commerce. They are good in buying and selling. This has enabled them occupy desirable positions in commercial spaces wherever they find themselves. Lagos, the commercial hub of Nigeria, is a typical example where Igbos enjoy dominance in trading. They control majority share of various segments of the major open markets. This is a glaring fact.

I have also taken time to explore the reason for this success and found out that one of the reasons is in the local expression: ONYE AHIAM. This is translated in English as, "My customer." The Igbos use an apprentice system of learning to train newcomers to trade. Young people or newcomers are trained and exposed to the rudiments of the trade for a particular period of time before establishing their own. The expression, ONYE AHIAM, is taught to the apprentice during this period of learning and they are made to understand that the life of the business depends on the ability to attract and sustain more customers.

The term, ONYE AHIAM, becomes a guiding principle. The apprentice would wish that every buyer repeats the buying experience. The expression achieves two major goals:

[1] It awakens the consciousness of the seller to do those things that will ensure a repeat purchase because he wants to sustain the patronage.

[2] It gladdens the heart of the buyer when he is referred to as ONYE AHIAM. People want to be recognized. The term serves as a bond between the buyer and the seller.

Again, each time the term is used, the buyer feels important.

The concept of ONYE AHIAM can be applied in every sales arena; whether you are selling products or services. Attracting customers is the first major function of the business and identifying ways of keeping them is another major aspect. The salesperson should research his customers or prospects with a view to discovering the best strategies that will ensure repeat patronage. Salespeople should discover why people buy or why previous customers stopped buying from them. Buyers don't just buy; they buy for one reason or the other. Consistent patronage doesn't just happen, it happens for one reason or the other. It is the duty of the sales and marketing people to find out why and how people buy. This is a fundamental assignment.

Start applying the concept of ONYE AHIAM which creates a paradigm that reminds you that the customer is the king. Let salespeople begin to create a system that will close gaps with the buyers. Always ensure that the gap between the buying and selling is brought closer each business day. Get connected with the customer or the prospect. Let the salesman see this as a way of life. Let the business as an entity embrace this model, because the customer will always remain The King!

KEEP CONNECTING

Developing relationship is a great attitude. Business relationship founded on long standing friendship will likely outlive the founders. Building bridges instead of walls will go a long way to sustain any form of relationship; whether in business or in personal life. The more you find ways to reach out to people and develop ties with them, the more you discover them.

Sociology teaches that man is a *social animal*. This means that man wants to communicate, relate and share with one another. No man is an island; this is an old wise saying.

Typical questions for you as a salesman are: How do you relate with your customers? How do you sustain the relationship you think you have developed? Do you really know the prospects you want to attract? If yes, what are you doing to ensure that they keep believing in you? Do you think the people who bought today may decide to buy from another source tomorrow? If you think so, what are you doing to ensure that you remain the first choice when buying comes to their mind? These are questions begging for answers!

The first approach to these questions is to put yourself in the buyer's shoes. Create in your mind a situation where you are the buyer and someone else is the seller. What will make you buy; what will make you continue to buy? Would you buy and repeat the buying experience if your expectations were not met? If the answer is no, then do those things you believe would sustain continued patronage.

What most buyers want is recognition. They want you to acknowledge the fact that they are patronizing your business; even when they have variety of choices to make. Recognizing a customer's patronage can be done in various ways. Saying the two magic words THANK YOU, can go a long way to express gratitude each time the customer buys. Keeping in touch with the customer could also be a great technique. Calling a customer on his birthday to wish him well goes a long way too. Gifts from sales or marketing people to their customers are always appreciated. Customers cherish these gifts because the message sends a positive signal that they are cherished.

The relationship between a salesperson and the buyer is vital. If the relationship is cordial enough, the salesperson and the buyer will be happy. Most salespeople take selling for granted, they think the customer must buy from them. They fail to see reasons they should put more efforts in developing a good relationship with the customer. The effort a salesperson put into attracting a customer should be enough to make him work harder in keeping that customer.

As expressed earlier in this book, Attracting, Sustaining and Expanding the customer base is a vital aspect of selling; it is the life of the business. It tells a business that will live and the one that will not. It also tells the business that will meet its target and the ones that will not. The importance of attracting, sustaining and expanding customers cannot be over emphasized. It is vital in the life of the business. Businesses should also keep track of its customers if they want to maintain a good relationship with them.

One of the major challenges salespeople encounter is keeping track of their customers. You cannot appraise if you don't have detailed information. You cannot evaluate if you don't know where you are coming from. It is when you have the statistics of the people buying and the ones you are yet to convert to customers - that you will be equipped with the best winning strategies. It is always said that you start from the known to the unknown.

Develop daily, weekly or monthly sales plan and assign relevant numbers to them. You need to know the details of people buying today, the ones you are prospecting and the customers who stopped buying. If you have these numbers, you will be better positioned to know how to keep in touch with them. Make out time to keep in touch with your customers; this shouldn't only be when you are selling to them. You have not done anything extraordinary if you see your customers only when you are selling to them; you will be going the extra mile when you keep in touch with them outside business periods. When you call or visit your customers to check how they are doing, you are investing in that business relationship. This type of call or visit shows that you like the customer and are ready to invest in the business relationship. It tells that you want to know what is happening in the customer's life and business. Keeping in touch with the customer or prospect should not only occur when you are closing a deal. It should be part of your routine; it should be a salesman's attitude.

THE SEED GROWS WHEN IRRIGATED

I was taught in Agricultural Science that irrigation is used in assisting the growth of agricultural crops, revegetation and maintenance of landscape. It is the artificial application of water to the soil or land to assist growth of crops especially where natural rainfall is insufficient to support growth of crops.

The message to take home from this definition is that farmers have devised ways to make the land richer and better in order to enable a bountiful harvest. They have had to go the extra mile to ensure achieving their aim of growing their crops. You must find a way to get desired results. I often say that if you can't think outside the box, break the box and start afresh!

The concept of irrigation is a good example of doing something extra to ensure that the best results are achieved. Farmers in this context have the choice of sitting down in their comfort zones and waiting only on natural rainfall to grow their crops. Nothing great happens within the comfort zone. You must step out of your comfort zone to fix stuff - just like the farmers who did something extraordinary by seeking external support through irrigation. Successful people look for ways to get things done. Average people look for the next excuse to give for their failure!

> *Successful people look for ways to get things done. Average people look for the next excuse to give for their failure!*

This illustration could also apply to the everyday life of the salesman. Every salesperson wishes to retain his or her customers, this is natural; I believe. The question now is what are the salespeople doing to keep their customers, how are they *irrigating* their customer base? What are they doing at every moment to grow their customers or prospects?

You need to sow before you reap. You need to work for people before you get their support. You need to have a proven track record of performance before you can attract people to be interested in you. The farmer needs to make the soil rich before he expects bountiful harvest; the richer the soil, the better the harvest. These are natural sequences. This concept applies in our daily lives. You need to create the world you desire.

I usually advise politicians to live like salespeople who wish to sell to customers always. The more the salesman delights the customer, the more the customer buys from the salesman. Politicians need to take time daily to affect people positively if they want votes from them. A salesman won't deceive his customer because he would want to sell to him again tomorrow. Successful salesmanship is hinged on attitude, truthfulness, relationship and value. These are the things that will attract patronage and customer loyalty. Same way, politicians should say what they will do and do what they said they will do.

I believe that performance is reality. Whenever you perform, the result will speak for you. Your performance will be your judge. People will seek you wherever you are and identify with you. People want to identify with success and excellent performance; people celebrate success. I am not saying that we don't have politicians who are reliable. I have met quite a few of them; I have seen politicians with great character. The question is, Are they in the majority? You give me the answer!

Now let us come back to our discussion. How have you *watered your soil* as a salesman? How have you invested in your customer, do you think it's "a one way traffic?" Every relationship needs to be nurtured; it needs to be invested in. It shouldn't be one sided; it should be of mutual benefit.

I recently listened to one of John C. Maxwell's leadership series where he explained that his goal is to add value to people. He explained his commitment to add value to leaders in order to multiply value to others. He asked the following questions during the session: What are you doing to invest in yourself? What have you done to invest in others? Have you been betting on yourself? He concluded his message with this thought, "I want to make a difference with people who want to make a difference doing something that makes a difference." I agree totally with this global authority. In order to make a real difference in life, you should learn how to invest in other people.

Zig Ziglar puts it this way, "*You can have everything you want in life, if you just help other people get what they want.*" The more you help other people to grow, the more you build your influence zone. Customers are tough and also easy to manage, it depends on the way you see it. You can make yours easy or tough. What you give is usually what you get. The level of what you will get in a venture is often a function of what you have invested in that project. If you cherish a customer to the extent that you see the customer as a friend, a family, or a partner, the customer will also see you that way. What you give is what you get. This is natural.

Most of the big accounts I sold to during my days in the field as a salesman were the customers I invested my time in their personal or professional development. I go out of my way to give professional counsel on what will work in their businesses. I organized free one-on-one coaching sessions for them just to make sure they grow in their businesses. My sales figures subsequently soared higher and higher. People will naturally want to repay good deeds. This is what the Law of Reciprocity I talked about earlier teaches. People will want to repay you for your good deeds to them. They will even want to do more than you did for them.

Take out time and add value to your customer. Stop selling for once and begin to invest in your customers! Lead your customers into new ways of succeeding in their areas if you can. Help them in any way you can; invest your time in them. Develop this attitude and start making a difference. Don't just see the relationship with the customer as one that ends up in writing an invoice. Closing sales is good but ensuring a

> The relationship will bring the sale. It will sustain it also.

healthy relationship with the customer or prospect is better. The relationship will bring the sale. It will sustain it also.

Invest something great in the relationship; the level of what you have invested will determine the stage you will get to in any form of relationship. Begin now to irrigate the relationship. Don't be like some politicians who only remember the electorate when election is close by. Be a successful salesman who remembers his customers when he is selling and when he is not. Let your customers see you as someone sent from above to help them grow. You attain this level of relationship with the customer only when you are willing to pay the price. The price is not costly; the price is irrigating the ground. The price is investing in the customer. This is the way to be successful in your sales career.

THE PLACE OF CUSTOMER RELATIONSHIP MANAGEMENT

One of my best quotes whenever I talk about the customer is the one from Peter Drucker, "*Quality in a service or product is not what you put into it. It is what the customer or client gets out of it.*" This thought is also my guide when I transact with customers. If you don't want to end up in a one-off sale, then let the customer be the centre of the business; let your customers have a feeling of satisfaction each time they buy from you.

Katherine Barchetti once said: "*Make a customer, not a sale.*" When you make a customer, the success of the business is guaranteed. The thing that guarantees the existence of the business is your ability in generating and keeping customers.

Our company's promise, "We Don't Only Satisfy Our Clients; We Delight Them," has put us on constant check to go beyond satisfying to delighting our customers. When you exceed the expectations of a Customer, he gets delighted. A Satisfied or Delighted Customer will not only repeat the purchase, he will become a promoter of your products or services. He will become *a moving billboard* for your organization. He sings your song everywhere he goes. Delighting your customers is the best customer relationship strategy.

The place of the customer in the success of the business is irreplaceable. Try to go the extra mile for the customer. Consider the customer when you are taking vital business decisions. Create in your subconscious mind where you imagine the customer as a member of the board where business decisions are taken. When you create this mind picture, the customer becomes the king. The customer will be king because every decision taken at the board meeting will have the customer in mind. Decision on production, sales and marketing, administration, operations, etc, will be taken from a view point that the customer is part of the decision, thus making the customer a vital factor in the organization.

Your duty as a salesman is to sell successfully by ensuring happy customers. Ensure your methods of selling will keep the customer. If you are a good salesman, you can sell any product or service to anyone once. This is certain but what is not guaranteed is a repeat purchase. It is your approach that will determine if there would be a repeat purchase or not.

The main goal of customer relationship management strategies is to ensure a bond with the customer; either when the customer is buying or after buying the product.

In the course of my career as a salesman, I have mentored a lot of people. I meet a lot of businesspeople and professionals. I like assessing people from the angle of how they value relationships. I look out to see what they do to keep great relationships. I also observe what they do to desire a business relationship.

Attracting customers requires a lot of work, so concerted effort should be taken to ensure that they are sustained. Keeping a customer can be likened to getting to the top. It takes more effort to stay at the top than climbing to the top. Staying successful in business requires more energy than all efforts expended to get to the top position. To stay successful in business, you need to be ahead of your competitors, you need to be innovative to stay up to date in order to delight your customers. You need to be steps ahead of competition in order to maintain relevance in your industry.

When you attract a customer, you must be seen to be doing things that will ensure a repeat purchase. You must treat the customer in a way that when he leaves your premises, he is sure to convince other people to patronize your business.

Don't stop thinking new ways to delight your customers. Develop new ways to make them happy. A happy customer is the strength of any business. A satisfied customer tells at least ten other people about your business. A delighted customer stays with the business and becomes an advocate who does not receive salary or sales commission! A delighted customer promotes your business; he tells everyone about your business, he becomes a great voice for the business.

BE CONSISTENT

On 26th September, 2018, I went to sell Nigeria Sales Conference to my friend and cerebral sales expert, Damola Akindolire, Executive Director, Sales, at Alpha Mead Development Company, leading Real Estate Company in Nigeria. Damola started by congratulating our company for winning the Top 100 Emerging SMEs in Nigeria and said to me, "The Selling Champion, you don't preach to the Choir! Coming from you, I know the Sales Conference will be a great event; we are coming to the conference!" Nothing beats performance on the negotiation table. If you know your job, if you are consistent in giving value; folks will speak in your favour.

> Nothing beats performance on the negotiation table. If you know your job, if you are consistent in giving value; folks will speak in your favour.

Walt Disney once said *"Do what you do so well that they want to see it again and bring their friends."* You have to be seen to be doing what you do greatly and repeatedly. Excellence is a virtue. You must embrace excellence if you want to remain a strong player in your profession. Excellence should be a consistent attitude in your company.

Successful companies are those that have demonstrated the attitude of consistency more than their competitors. Consistency should be the character of your company. Organizations should be consistent in offering high quality products and services. They should be consistent in hiring the best staff in their industry. They should be consistent in training and retraining their personnel. They should be seen to be consistent in ensuring excellent service delivery.

Ensuring repeat purchase or referral is not the duty of salespeople alone. It is a collective responsibility, but with sales and marketing people at the forefront. The entire system in an organization should function as a whole towards actualizing the concept of consistency. All the departments should work together from a mindset that the customer is the reason they gathered in the first place. The accounts department gets figures to calculate because a sale has taken place. The Human Resources department hires personnel because it is believed that the business would be patronized by customers. The company won't be able to pay salaries or remunerations if such patronage fails to occur. Every department in the organization gets busy because a customer has patronized the business. Customer service therefore is not a department; it is everyone's job! Every Personnel in the Organization should develop this mindset.

Consistency in service delivery goes a long way to ensure customer loyalty. Don't be seen to be inconsistent. Let your word be your bond. Let what you say be what you do. Create a unique system. Customers want to get value for their money. In some cases, they want to get more value than they have paid for, and they want the company to give this value all the time. This is a fact of today's business.

The customer is faced with a lot of products and choices. Businesses have a lot of attractive offerings for buyers. The business arena is stiff and meant for prepared folks. Businesses that are consistent in value delivery are the *players* that will succeed in this competitive business arena.

The salesman who is able to show that he can give value over and over again will always win the hearts of his customers. Being consistent in doing the things that will bring the customers back is a great approach. The formula to achieving this is simple. Try to repeat what makes the customer happy! Whenever the buyer expresses satisfaction for an action; try to repeat the action again. You make a strong statement each time you delight the customer. The customer will come again with great expectations to receive or exceed the previous experience.

In order to be a successful salesman, you need to make happy customers who are willing to buy, and being consistent in efficient service delivery is one of the strategies to achieving this. Happy customers are repeat customers and repeat customers stay with the business for a long time. Happy customers are the most sought after type of customers because they buy most of the time. You don't spend your entire budget trying to attract them. They buy because someone has made them to continue in the buying experience. Their continuous patronage is hinged on the amount of efforts that is invested to make them consistently happy.

The Art of Selling is a journey and not a destination. You are required to keep getting better. You are expected to keep improving in knowledge. You are expected to be innovative. You are required to keep delighting your customers and prospects. Your products and services must be outstanding. The marketplace is highly demanding and you must be up-to-date and equipped to take your rightful place in the market.

It is my desire that you put into practice the recommendations in this book.

Happy Selling!

Rule1: The customer is always right. Rule 2: If the customer is ever wrong, re-read Rule 1 -Stew Leonard

SALES TIPS

1. Don't only develop customers. Work hard to keep them.
2. Always remember that if you don't sell "Yes" to the customer; you buy "No" from him!
3. Your selling is not successful until there is a repeat purchase or referral.
4. Always sell for the next invoice.
5. Develop happy customers. They are like diamonds.
6. Get personal with your customers. It makes you smile to the bank!
7. Be Extraordinary! Normal doesn't sell anymore.
8. Always put yourself in the customers' shoes. It makes you serve them better.
9. Go the extra mile for the customer. This is the way to become a selling champion.
10. Don't stop thinking new ways to delight the customer. Innovation beats competition!

Whatever you believe with feelings becomes your reality.
  – Brian Tracy

OTHER BOOKS BY GEORGE O. EMETUCHE

THE SELLING CHAMPION

The 11 Irrefutable Principles Of Success

EVERYTHING IS POSSIBLE!

THE 25 UNBREAKABLE LAWS OF SALES

SUCCEEDING WITH YOUR SPOUSE

BE INSPIRED!

FOR SALES TRAINING OR BULK PURCHASE OF OUR BOOKS OR CDs, PLEASE CONTACT:

THE SELLING CHAMPION CONSULTING LIMITED:
sales@thesellingchampionconsulting.com

OR VISIT:
www.thesellingchampionconsulting.com

OR CALL:
08186083133, 07060559429

www.ingramcontent.com/pod-product-compliance
Lightning Source LLC
Chambersburg PA
CBHW060828220526
45466CB00003B/1026